"Have you found a sacred space, a Shiloh, a Jerusalem, where the living God reveals himself and speaks tenderly to you? Hearson demonstrates how the 'sacred space' tradition evolved throughout Israel's history, beginning with the garden of Eden and concluding with the everlasting Temple in heaven. On Mt Sinai, at Bethel, at Gilgal, and in numerous other hallowed places, God visited his people with blessings and/or judgment. With the advent of Jesus, believers have become holy temples, sacred places where God dwells, speaks, and reveals himself. This book invites you to live as the temple of the Holy Spirit, as a place where God yearns to commune intimately with you."

—**Hélène Dallaire**, Earl S. Kalland Professor of Old
Testament and Semitic Languages, Denver Seminary

"The prophet Jeremiah offers a stern warning to the inhabitants of Jerusalem: repent or become like Shiloh. On the one hand Shiloh serves as the prophetic paradigm for the consequences of neglecting the word of the Lord. On the other hand, its divine abandonment offers solace for believers today because it serves as a reminder that God's presence is not relegated to a geographical 'holy' site. Rather, God's name resides where he chooses it to dwell, whether in a city, a temple, or in the lives of the faithful. With acute attention to the biblical text and an astute eye on its theological ramifications, Hearson demonstrates how an understanding of sacred space in the biblical world has profound implications for understanding how God continues to connect with all who call upon his name."

—**Kyle R. Greenwood**, administrative director, MA programs,
Development Associates International; associated professor
of Old Testament, Denver Seminary; and adjunct associate
professor of Old Testament, Fuller Theological Seminary

"The themes of divine and sacred presence and space and their various expressions are pivotal concepts for historical, literary, and theological narratives in both the Old Testament and New Testament. After evaluating sacred sites like Bethel, Beersheba, Gilgal, and Shiloh (from sacralization to desacralization), Dr. Hearson, in a clear and persuasive manner, demonstrates how these grand themes of biblical theology find their epicenter in the Jerusalem Temple in the Old Testament and Messiah Jesus in the New Testament. Hearson's research and foray into these complicated ideas provides both the student and seasoned reader of Scripture a detailed exploration of God's sacred presence and geography and their ultimate culmination in Jesus as sacred space."

—**James F. Linzey**, chief editor, Modern English Version Bible

"As a pastor it can be challenging to communicate in a way that connects with all people along a broad spectrum of biblical understanding. Blake Hearson's use of metaphors and analogies in *Go Now to Shiloh* meets the challenge of communicating well with a wide range of readers. Before journeying back to Bethel, Gilgal, the burning bush, or the tabernacle, he takes his reader first to Gettysburg and Ground Zero to illustrate the concept of sacred space. His use of telegram, cell phone, and phone booth metaphors weave throughout his survey of Old Testament sacred spaces to help illustrate how God interacted with his people at each stop along the way. *Go Now to Shiloh* takes deep dives into each sacred space in a way that unlocks new insights for seasoned Bible scholars, but does so in a way that does not leave the novice reader behind. He paints a beautiful picture of how God moves from sacred space to sacred person when the 'Stargates' of old had been destroyed. *Go Now to Shiloh* provides both a deeper understand of the concept of sacred space, as well as a deeper appreciation for how God communicates with his sacred people."

—**Matt Marrs**, Send Network Regional Director–
Midwest, North American Mission Board, and lead pastor,
Northland Baptist Church, Kansas City, MO

"*Go Now to Shiloh* is essential reading for anyone who is interested in communicating with God and understanding how and where God presents himself. Drawing on his doctoral research at Hebrew Union College, N. Blake Hearson identifies the different kinds of sacred spaces God chooses from Genesis to Revelation, and he explains them in accessible and creative ways. This book inspires me to know God on his own terms and to thrive in God's presence and self-revelation."

—**Kenneth C. Way**, associate professor and chair of Old Testament
and Semitics, Talbot School of Theology, Biola University

GO

NOW

TO

SHILOH

GO
NOW
TO
SHILOH

A Biblical Theology of Sacred Space

N. BLAKE HEARSON

B&H
ACADEMIC
NASHVILLE, TENNESSEE

ISBN: 978-0-8054-4883-2

Dewey Decimal Classification: 231.74
Subject Heading: BIBLE--GEOGRAPHY / GOD / REVELATION

Scripture taken from the NEW AMERICAN STANDARD BIBLE®,
Copyright © 1960, 1962, 1963, 1968, 1971, 1972, 1973, 1975,
1977, 1995 by The Lockman Foundation. Used by permission.

Cover design by Emily Keafer Lambright.
Cover Art: Vintage Wood Engraving from 1886, via iStock.

Printed in the United States of America

1 2 3 4 5 6 7 8 9 10 VP 25 24 23 22 21 20

Dedicated to my wife, Jennifer, without whom none of this would have been possible. Your sacrificial support has been a wonderful gift of love.

TABLE OF CONTENTS

ACKNOWLEDGEMENTS

The study you have before you has its origins in the juxtaposition of two texts. I have had a long-standing interest in the first text, the so-called "temple sermon" of Jeremiah 7. The prophet's condemnation of the worship going on at the temple in Jerusalem is fascinating when set against the account of the miraculous deliverance of the city and its temple from the Assyrian invasion in 2 Kings 19. It is easy to see why Jeremiah's audience expects another divine intervention for the city. However, I find it equally fascinating that Shiloh, a former sanctuary that was later destroyed, is used as the means of comparison for the temple in Jerusalem. What was the initial relationship between Shiloh and God, and how did that change so that the city later served as an example in the prophecy of the doom of Jerusalem?

The second passage was brought to my attention by the late Dr. David Weisberg of Hebrew Union College and comes from the rabbinic text *Mishnah Zevahim* 14:5–8. This passage lists a number of sites, coupled with a declaration of whether or not high places were permitted or forbidden at those locations. The sites seem to represent periods of Israelite history connected to the movements of the tabernacle and ark. Jerusalem is, of course, the end and pinnacle of the list. However, the one site that parallels Jerusalem in the list is Shiloh. In the Jeremiah passage, there is no implication that Shiloh was destroyed because of Jerusalem or even to make way for the primacy of Jerusalem. Rather, Shiloh is the example for Jerusalem, implying that at one time Shiloh had a similar level of significance to Jerusalem and yet was not immune to destruction. This led me to ask: what gave Shiloh a significance that would make it comparable to

Jerusalem in status, and what, in the perspective of the biblical narrative, led to its destruction? Furthermore, and perhaps more importantly, how did the loss of these places impact communication with God?

The end result of these thoughts and questions is the study you have before you. Before proceeding, I must address what is perhaps the most important part of any large work: acknowledgments and thanks. First and foremost, I want to thank my wife, Jennifer. She has stood by me through the long and seemingly endless process of writing. Anyone who has success-fully completed a book knows that its demands often extend beyond the writer to his family. She even served as an editor, giving of her own time to read through the drafts of this work. I can truly say that I could not have completed this project without her help and support. Her endurance has truly been a gift of love.

I owe a deep debt of gratitude to the late Dr. David Weisberg for his encouragement and help in the initial stages of this project. He was one of the kindest and most thoughtful people I have had the privilege of knowing and the world is most diminished for no longer having his presence in it. Likewise, this project would have failed to get out of the gate without Dr. Richard Sarason's detailed and kind help. He went above and beyond in every way to help me get the project into its initial form as a dissertation. He is a scholar and gentlemen in the truest sense of the words. Both of these men gave me tremendous support and help in hammering out the para-meters and approach of the study.

I want to express my deep gratitude to my parents, Les and Pat Hearson, for their love and encouragement. They supported me emotionally, finan-cially, and spiritually throughout all my years of education and beyond in any way they could. Their steady belief in my ability to accomplish the task made an incalculable impact on me. I am one of the fortunate few who have in his or her parents two very good friends. Even though my mother is now with her beloved Jesus, I know in my heart that this book would please her to no end.

Over the years, my various graders have done the yeoman's work of helping with editing. Most recently, Garrett Skrbina and William "Trey" Bechtold have given me a great deal of help. Their insights and aid saved me hours of work and from more than a few mistakes. They are representative of a promising future for scholarship and service for Christ's church and kingdom. To the many other students who contributed along the way, either via editing work or discussions, I thank you.

I would be remiss if I didn't thank two of my colleagues as well. Dr. Thor Madsen gave freely from his busy schedule to help make suggestions and edits in those places where the words just didn't work. Additionally, both he and Dr. Rustin Umstattd spent time discussing the ideas in the book that helped me refine my thoughts. Their friendship and collegiality are a great blessing.

Of course, no book sees the light of day without the capable help of a team at the book's publisher. Most recently, Audrey Greeson, Sarah Landers, and Jessi Wallace have been a tremendous help in finalizing the process. Yet I also know there is a whole host of people who are involved behind the scenes. Thus, my deepest appreciation goes out to the team at B&H for all of their gracious help!

Last but far from least, I want to thank my daughters, Emma and Claire. They have helped me in the way that only children can: by reminding me of what is truly important in life. There is nothing quite as refreshing as the laughter and freely given love of one's child.

All of these people—my own little community—have contributed in ways large and small to the success of this project. I cannot thank them enough for their help. Where the research and conclusions have met with success, I owe them the thanks. Any shortcomings or errors that remain are solely my own.

N. Blake Hearson
Kansas City, Missouri

ABBREVIATIONS

ANET	*Ancient Near Eastern Texts*
BA	*Biblical Archaeologist*
BASOR	*Bulletin of the American Schools of Oriental Research*
BHS	*Biblia Hebraica Stuttgartensia*
Bib	Biblica
BR	*Bible Review*
BTB	*Biblical Theology Bulletin*
CAD	*Chicago Assyrian Dictionary*
CBQ	*Catholic Biblical Quarterly*
CCR	*Coptic Church Review*
Di	Dialogue
ETL	*Ephemerides Theologicae Lovanienses*
ExpTim	*Expository Times*
GKC	*Gesenius' Hebrew Grammar*
HBT	*Horizons in Biblical Theology*
HR	*History of Religions*
HTR	*Harvard Theological Review*
HUCA	*Hebrew Union College Annual*
JAAR	*Journal of the American Academy of Religion*
JAOS	*Journal of the American Oriental Society*
JBL	*Journal of Biblical Literature*
JCS	*Journal of Cuneiform Studies*
JJS	*Journal of Jewish Studies*
JNES	*Journal of Near Eastern Studies*

JPS	Jewish Publication Society
JQJ	*Judaism, A Quarterly Journal*
JQR	*Jewish Quarterly Review*
JR	*Journal of Religion*
JSJ	*Journal for the Study of Judaism*
JSOT	*Journal for the Study of the Old Testament*
JSS	*Journal of Semitic Studies*
JTS	*Journal of Theological Studies*
NASB	New American Standard Bible (1995)
NIBT	*New International Bible Commentary*
NIV	New International Version
OTWSA	Ou-Testamentiese Werkgemeenskap in Suider Africa
Parab	*Parabola*
PEQ	*Palestinian Exploration Quarterly*
Proof	*Prooftexts: A Journal of Jewish Literary History*
RB	*Revue Biblique*
Sem	*Semitica*
SR	*Studies in Religion*
Trad	*Tradition*
TynBul	*Tyndale Bulletin*
VT	*Vetus Testamentum*
VTSupp	Supplements to Vetus Testamentum
ZAW	*Zeitschrift für die alttestamentliche Wissenschaft*

INTRODUCTION

In many ways, the story of sacred places in the Bible is the story of divine and human efforts to restore what was lost when mankind was ejected from the Garden. While God has always made himself available to those who seek him, communication was not always guaranteed before the advent of Jesus and his saving work. More precisely, whether or not God would receive the message of the one seeking him was often in doubt. This uncertainty is especially evident when one considers the need for sacrifices and proper procedure in order for a sinful human being to encounter a holy God. Interaction with God after the fall came at the cost of life (Gen 3:21). Yet grace has always been a part of God's character, and he has always made a way.

God provided a way, for instance, when he selected a few individuals who had access to him in special ways and at particular places. From Abraham to Moses, God would show up and speak with special people and make arrangements through these people for communication with many more. We see an ebb and flow in the story of God's communication with humanity—this story includes periods of seeming silence from God followed by periods of frequent communication. There were even times when mankind tried to force God's hand by reaching him. Most of us are familiar with the famous example of this attempt when the people tried to reach heaven via the Tower of Babel. Yet, as the builders of the tower would discover, human beings can only approach God on his own terms. Thus, even during times of greater self-revelation by God, his communication often occurred at specific places with specific people. Places like Shiloh, Bethel, Beersheba, and Sinai all served as meeting grounds between heaven and earth, between God and man. The close connection, lost when God banished Adam and Eve from the Garden, would be partly restored in the form of these other sacred places. These places can be thought of as phone booths that God established for interaction with him. A barrier remained because of sin, but communication was possible.

The book you have before you investigates such places and meeting grounds between God and his chosen people, giving most of its attention to the Old Testament. It examines how God made himself available for fellowship before, and in ways that even foreshadow, Jesus's work on the cross. It will examine how these places came to be sacred and the circumstances that led to their being de-sanctified and, for that reason, no longer effective as places to meet God. As a larger effect, our study will underscore the value and importance of communication with God, as it demonstrates the struggle faced by humanity in having this communication restored. As a starting point, we will look at the challenges involved in the effort to communicate with a holy God. Then we will consider what is meant by "sacred space," giving special care to contrast the biblical notion of sacred space with ideas found in surrounding cultures, which may be superficially similar to the biblical view. This general concept will support the next step, which involves the idea of temporary sacred space, the most familiar example being the sanctity of the ground beneath Moses's feet. Subsequent material will address, for example, the tabernacle, enduring sacred spaces, the human impact on the rejection of sacred space, and the direct measures taken by God to create new lifelines between himself and his people. In each case, we will discover afresh the grace of God, as the loss of one sacred space gives way to new expressions of intimacy. Ultimately God always provides a way to have fellowship with him, even though sin bars the way.

The present study is, therefore, all about places and the God who makes himself known and available therein. But in a larger sense, we trust that it will provide the reader with a deeper understanding of who God is and who we are, as his beloved but fallen creatures.

CHAPTER 1

IN THE BEGINNING

Communicating with God in the Bible

On November 19, 1863, Abraham Lincoln gave a few short remarks at the dedication of the battlefield at Gettysburg. His remarks, while brief, pointed to bloodshed as the cause that sanctified this ordinary field. Somehow, the loss of so many lives in that epic struggle changed the grass and soil, turning these elements and this place into a national monument that is honored to this day. After the intense three-day conflict, the area would never be the same. Add to this the dedication of the area as a final resting place for those who died in the fight, and the result is sacred ground. An ordinary space became extraordinary and off-limits to most everyday activities. Today, this site is visited by thousands annually, even after 150 years.

Fast-forward now to September 11, 2001. Early in the morning, on an ordinary Tuesday, several acres of land became sacrosanct, once again through the shedding of blood. Terrorists hijacked four passenger jets and used them as bombs against the United States. The two planes that flew into the Twin Towers of the World Trade Center in Lower Manhattan created the most death and destruction. After the attack was over, the debris of the towers was cleared away, and the human remains interred, discussions began as to what to do with "ground zero" where the buildings had stood. As with

Gettysburg, the sheer number of lives lost changed the nature of the space where the Twin Towers once stood.

Strangely, American Christians generally do not see their church buildings as sacred spaces. We have some sense of things that we may not do in a church, but these boundaries more reflect ideas of politeness than beliefs as to what mysterious happenings occur there. If a church burns down, whether by accident or by an act of hatred, we view it as a tragedy for the congregation. The community that met in that church is deeply saddened by the loss. But no one in that congregation considers himself cut off from God. After all, the church is a body of believers, not a building. If anything, the loss of the building may bring the congregation closer as they pray together and seek to rebuild. We do not view the loss as a curse on a sacred place that makes it unfit for another church building. On the contrary, we depend upon the fact that contact with God remains unbroken.

Similarly, when a congregation dwindles and they sell their property, there is no caveat on how that property may be used. I have personally seen churches become bookstores, pubs, coffee shops, and even furniture outlets. While Christians may experience a sense of sadness to see their former churches used in these ways, they do not sense that sacred space has been violated. Neither the building nor the location contributed to the ability of people to communicate with God in that place.

Yet, our beliefs about sacred spaces were not always the norm. In fact, the Israelite of the Old Testament and the Jew of the New Testament would have found our notions strange—even perverse. God had revealed himself to them at particular places, and proper worship of and contact with him had to happen there. Part of this idea was linked to the need for sacrifices, but it was also ingrained in the theology of the entire Bible, with analogies found in other religions.[1] As we will see below, even the Garden of Eden was such a place; it was the meeting ground between Adam, Eve, and God.

---

[1] Eliade's work sheds valuable light on this subject. He argues that across religious systems, a profane (i.e., ordinary) space became sacred when a divine being manifested itself there. The actions of men played no role in the sanctity of

A metaphor is useful here. When I was growing up, the primary means of communication with anyone at a distance was a landline phone. If you were away from home and were in public space, you would look for a phone booth. You would step into the little cubicle, close the door, put in some change, and make a call. Even when Commissioner Gordon had to reach Batman, he used either the Bat Signal or a special phone. Cell phones, email, and texting were not options at that point.

Sacred spaces in the Old Testament tended to function in much the same way. If a worshiper wanted assurance of contact with God, he had to find a "phone booth" to reach him. God was everywhere, of course, but because of the fall, he was not everywhere *reachable*. Although communication remained difficult, God had set up access points or, in our analogy, phone booths, where his worshipers could have assurance of reaching him. It is important to note that these sacred places did not come about by some catastrophe like 9/11. Rather, God revealed *himself* at the sometimes-surprising locations. Much like phone booths, the connection could also be lost. Just as our phone companies might remove pay phones, so God might remove our means to connect with him and replace it with another.

To use a second analogy, it may be helpful to think of these connection points between heaven and earth as "stargates."[2] Science fiction fans will know that some worlds contain stargates linking one place (or time) to another far away. In the movie *Stargate*, a gate is discovered that allows humans to travel vast distances through space to another planet.[3] The story reveals that parasitic aliens built these gates to glean cheap labor and human hosts on earth. The gate was ultimately buried long ago, so that the aliens could no longer reach earth, but it is discovered again in modern times. In

---

a space. The holiest sites and temples in a system were considered the center of the world and provided an axis around which a people could orient their existence. See Mircea Eliade, *The Sacred and the Profane: The Nature of Religion* (New York: Harcourt, 1959).

[2] I am indebted to Rustin Umstattd for this analogy.

[3] *Stargate*, directed by Roland Emmerich (Beverly Hills, CA: Metro-Goldwyn-Mayer, 1994).

this case, the analogy of a stargate illustrates that there is a special connection that overcomes an otherwise insurmountable barrier to communication.

Naturally, all analogies have limits and fail at some points. We are limited, and so are our analogies. However, the analogy of phones as a means of communication remains helpful, and it will serve as our primary metaphor moving forward. As such, the reader will see the development of communication with God in the Bible following the analogy of landlines through the early stages of cell phones and up to their current widespread use. As a result, we will see just how amazing our level of access to God really is and appreciate it in a new way.

Defining Sacred Space in the Bible

How does the Bible depict sacred space? At the bare-bones level, *sacred space* is a place where God has declared himself accessible to the worshiper. It is thus set in contrast to all other places. Among biblical scholars who study sacred places in the Bible, the focus is often on worship at the temple in Jerusalem; this comes from the view that the authors of Scripture sought to isolate Jerusalem as the only holy place acceptable to God. While this assumption is partially accurate, it also invites the question: Why did Jerusalem become so important in the first place? The history of contact between heaven and earth shows that Jerusalem became important to the degree that other points of contact with God were lost (e.g., Num 33:52; Deut 7:5; 12:1–7; 1 Kgs 3:2–3; 8:5–11; 11:1–10). In other words, given this attrition in the number of communication points with God, the temple in Jerusalem became the last site standing, the last holdover phone booth. Attempts to reach God via other places were met with the message, "This number is no longer in service." Yet the focus on Jerusalem as the sole connection between God and his people causes us to miss the development of communication with a holy God in a fallen world. Furthermore, failing to observe the dynamics of fellowship and communion through sacred places causes us to miss the full effect of Jerusalem's destruction in the Old and New Testaments.

In order to understand how biblical sacred space developed and functioned, we must go back to creation itself. When looking at the idea of sacred space in the Bible, it is apparent that the created world in its entirety has some level of sacredness, simply as the handiwork of God. However, this is only one aspect of the biblical perspective. As noted above, the Bible also depicts specific sites as holy, given their use by God to meet with selected people. These places became holy because God revealed himself there; they were places where God was accessible to his people. *HalleluJAH!!*

As with most things, the story of God's communication with mankind starts in the garden of Eden. Most Christians are familiar with this story and focus on the goodness of creation, subsequently marred by the sin of Adam and Eve. While this emphasis is fitting, it should not overshadow other important truths. For example, we often miss the actual purpose of the garden itself. My students are always surprised to learn that Adam and Eve were not created in the garden; they were placed there after their creation (read carefully Gen 2:7–8).

The garden was a special place with a special purpose. Adam and Eve were given tasks in Eden that would mirror the work of God in creating the world, while meeting their practical needs. Still, the primary function of Eden was as a site for fellowship with God.[4] It was a place for God to commune and have harmonious relationship with beings made in his image. Thus, when Adam and Eve were banished from the garden, they were not just deprived of easy food and shelter; they also lost their interaction with God.   *Jesus!!*

This loss became evident when they ate the forbidden fruit. Their place of fellowship became a place of fear, and its plants were used for cover and concealment. When their sin became apparent, God stated that they could not continue in such a state; they had to suffer the loss of sustenance and ready access to him. Creation would now resist their efforts to communicate with him, so it is more than ironic that Adam and Eve hid from him as he sought them. They were afraid. Their communication with God had

---

[4] See G. K. Beale and Mitchell Kim, *God Dwells among Us: Expanding Eden to the Ends of the Earth* (Downers Grove, IL: InterVarsity Press, 2014).

already been disrupted. By consciously avoiding him, they revealed that his presence was now too difficult for them to take. God's nearness inspired guilt and fear.

When God cast Adam and Eve out of the garden, he was giving them what their actions demanded: separation from God. Anyone who has had a falling out with a friend or spouse knows how difficult it is to be in the same room with that person. At the very least, it is awkward, and at worst, it is intolerable. Nothing can be enjoyed without resolution of the conflict or removal from the shared location. Thus, we can see how much greater the friction was between a holy God and his rebellious creatures. The initial solution was a change of venue for those creatures.

Yet this change of location, and resulting limitation of communication, did not really fix anything. The same awkwardness and pain remained. In human society, it is possible to escape our problems geographically. There are other places available to us and other people with whom to build positive relationships; not so with the Creator. Our relationship with him is inescapable. We will either seek restoration or spend a lifetime consciously or subconsciously avoiding him. There are no other options, and we know from the full revelation of Scripture that God desires restoration of both relationship and communication.

When Adam and Eve were ejected from the garden, they were removed from the discernable presence of God, but this loss does not imply that all communication with him was cut off. Rather, much like their relationship with the earth, interaction with each other, and ease of reproduction, communication only became much more difficult. Adam and Eve failed to submit to the authority of God, and that jeopardized their relationship with him. They lost the dedicated line to God and were forced into submission to his self-revelation in order to have fellowship with him.

As the Bible's story progresses, we see that particular places in the Bible would come to serve as stopgap measures for humanity's lost connection. No longer would God and mankind live under the same roof. Rather, the Creator would choose to communicate at exact times and places with no open-door policy. Meetings would occur by appointment and invitation

only. Ultimately, Jesus would change things with his advent on earth, but
the full restoration of what was lost in the garden remains to be fulfilled. *Amen.*
In the time between the loss of fellowship in the garden in Genesis and the
ultimate redemption of creation in Revelation, communication with God
is a difficult process. *my LORD!!*

The Tower of Babel illustrates the sin of do-it-yourself phone repair,
which God cannot abide. At its core, the story is about mankind's desire to
reach God physically and on equal terms. With respect to the latter, which
preoccupies many interpreters, the sin of the builders parallels the sin of
Adam and Eve. The builders wished to be independent of God and to throw
off the bonds of humility. To have access to God that was not dependent on
God's self-revelation meant reaching equality with him. Humanity would *uh oh!*
not be bound by God's will, if they could reach him at any time. However,
the modern interpreter often dismisses the importance of the tower's design.

The whole idea seems ludicrous to us. After all, in our world of sky-
scrapers, who would consider building a tower that could reach God? The
desire to build such a tower should alert the modern reader to the fundamentally different way that ancient peoples viewed the universe. In their
minds, God really could be physically reached; and if he could be reached,
he could be controlled or weakened. Of course, the story ends with God
foiling the plan of the people by making communication and fellowship
among themselves as difficult as communication with God had become.
The curse of the fall increased via greater difficulty in fellowship among
mankind. Communion with God was difficult because of the fall; communion between people became difficult because of the Tower of Babel.

To be sure, God did not desire for all communication between himself
and mankind to cease. By revealing himself at different times and places,
he created access points where people might still connect with him. For
example, in Exod 20:24, God stated in relation to sacrifice, "In every place
where I cause My name to be remembered, I will come to you and bless
you." In other words, God chose the places where an interaction with him
could occur. In terms of our analogy, God set up phone booths from which
he would receive calls. The presence of these places implied, to the biblical

Jesus!

any
of

authors, that all other places would not be appropriate for worship. Indeed, God made this rule clear in Deut 12:2–5. Thus, a sacred place was one that had some special association with God that consequently set it apart from the rest of the land.

Yet, even when a place was revealed as having a special connection with God, there was no guarantee that the connection would remain forever. When we look at the example of Shiloh in Jeremiah 7, we find that God's relationship with a particular sacred space can change. By the time of the prophet, Shiloh had been destroyed. Jeremiah related the words of God to the inhabitants of Jerusalem and declared, "Therefore, I will do to the house which is called by My name, in which you trust, and to the place which I gave you and your fathers, as I did to Shiloh" (Jer 7:14). Jeremiah attributed to God the destruction of these sanctified places. Just as God set up a phone booth, he could remove the line and terminate its connection.

Finally, even as modes of communication change and develop in modern society, so did the modes of communication with God. In order to understand how communication changed in the Bible, we will press our analogy. There are three primary ways of communication with God in the Bible, and they overlap with each other at some points. As we move through the story of the Bible, we will see that these three types of communication, or sacred spaces, are analogous to the functions of a phone booth, a telegram, and a cell phone.

Approaching the Study of Sacred Space

Before defining the types of sacred space that allow communication with God in the Bible, it is helpful to note that not everyone approaches the topic in the same way. Many studies on biblical texts, even if they subscribe to an entirely different approach to the sacred places, find themselves leaning on categories and terms found in the historical-critical method that pervades biblical scholarship; while it may be useful at points, the historical-critical method has not contributed significantly to the topic of sacred space in biblical literature. This lack is due to its goal of providing a "critically assured minimum" of historical reality.[5] In other words, the historical-critical approach tries to find the lowest common denominator that can be proven true against every form of scientific skepticism. As a product of the Enlightenment, the historical-critical method "views history as a closed continuum, an unbroken series of causes and effects in which there is no room for transcendence";[6] when this method is applied to the biblical text, it yields only fragmentary results and a distorted view of biblical theology.

Therefore, while sacred space as an idea is subject to historical analysis, and while the historical-critical methods answer some important questions,[7] they must give way to a larger effort to understand the relationship between God and earthly spaces theologically, since exegesis views the Bible as a cohesive and sacred Scripture. Accordingly, this book will examine the ideas that run through the Old Testament and, to a lesser degree, the New Testament, with the assumption that there is a divine author behind the text that gives the Bible unity of thought.[8]

This study will explore the issue of sacred space from a different angle than those typically taken by the more skeptical methods utilized in scholarship. We will look at a selection of several sites to determine why God rejected them and what caused the change in Israel's relationship with God to bring about their downfall. This method will offer fresh insight that goes beyond the focus on Jerusalem as the only proper place to worship.[9] Indirectly, this approach will offer new insight into the changing nature of God's relationship with the sacred space of Jerusalem. Ultimately, our study

---

[5] See Gerhard von Rad, *Old Testament Theology*, vol. 1 (Louisville, KY: John Knox, 2001), 108.

[6] Gerhard Hasel, *Old Testament Theology* (Grand Rapids: Eerdmans, 1991), 198. Naturally, this runs the danger of forcing ideas into a Procrustean bed.

[7] I am indebted to Dr. Richard Sarason for this idea.

[8] This approach is akin to Brevard Child's canonical approach, but does not dispense with historical veracity, as he does in his work. See Brevard Childs, *Old Testament Theology in a Canonical Context* (Philadelphia: Fortress, 1989).

[9] This approach also gives voice to the reasons conveyed in the biblical text, rather than leaning on the notion that the biblical authors are simply being clandestine about their favoritism of Jerusalem.

will give a better picture of the developing ideas and worldview surrounding
God's relationship with sacred spaces and how we communicate with God.

The present study is an exercise in biblical theology, with special attention to Old Testament theology. Thus, we take as our starting point the Old
Testament,[10] with only a brief look at the New Testament. The primary aim of
the study is to determine what ideas run through the entire Old Testament,[11]
with proper allowances made for the Old Testament's obvious literary features. The authors of the Bible give a record of events that are interpreted
through a theological understanding of their world. In our examination, we
will be dealing with the implied author and implied audience.[12]

Working with a method that is both theological and historical demands
the recognition of the relativity of any so-called human objectivity.[13] The
modern reader must realize that both he and the author make an indispens-
able contribution to interpretation. Additionally, the issue of identifying
authorial intent in the biblical material is fraught with difficulty.[14] Yet this
is true of any method or approach. For example, scholarship in the last
century and a half has endeavored to discover the "real" history behind the
narrative accounts of the Bible. This method usually translates into a picture

---

[10] Our approach will be similar to Sara Japhet's in Sara Japhet, "Some Biblical
Concepts of Sacred Place," in *Sacred Space: Shrine, City, Land*, ed. B. Z. Kedar
and R. J. Z. Werblowsky (New York: New York University Press, 1998), 55–72.

[11] This is a literary/canonical approach. For differing examples of this
approach, see Jack Miles, *God: A Biography* (New York: Alfred A. Knopf, 1995);
Brevard S. Childs, *Introduction to the Old Testament as Scripture* (Philadelphia:
Fortress, 1979); and *The Book of Exodus: A Critical Theological Commentary*
(Philadelphia: Westminster, 1974).

[12] In other words, the author as represented in the text and the assumed audi-
ence of the text. See Jonathan Culler, *Literary Theory: A Very Short Introduction*
(Oxford: Oxford University Press, 1997) and Gordon J. Wenham, *Story as Torah:
Reading the Old Testament Narrative Ethically* (Grand Rapids: Baker, 2000).

[13] See Hasel, *Old Testament Theology*, 200.

[14] See Wenham, *Story as Torah*, 7. Wenham discusses methodology with
respect to an ethical reading of the Old Testament narrative in which source
criticism is marginal since, whether the author was using three major sources or
"umpteen independent short stories," the message of the text is the same.

of the event as seen through the eyes of a post-Enlightenment scholar rather than the early readers of the text. Thus, such an approach is just as laden with interpretation; only the presuppositions are different. Our approach will not focus on this sort of re-creation of the event behind the narrative, since the concepts and perspectives within the Bible concerning God's relationship to sacred space are precisely what interest us. Approaching the issue of sacred space from this angle will give a fresh perspective and, hopefully, a better picture of how the authors of the ancient texts understood the relationship between God and their world.

The conclusions that we draw from the Old Testament will serve as the basis for a brief examination of select sources from the New Testament. The New Testament authors based their ideas on both the text of the Old Testament and on their own experience with the teachings of Jesus. Therefore, Old Testament ideas about sacred places will help us determine what the New Testament authors believed about God's changing relationship to sacred spaces. Finally, we will see that, for the New Testament authors, the loss of the temple in Jerusalem was equivalent to the loss of a connection with God. Such a loss could only be rectified by the work of Jesus.

Categories of Sacred Space in the Bible

Working from the above ideas, we can discern three subcategories of sacred spaces.[15] The first encompasses places that were only temporarily sacred during a divine revelation. These places are analogous to the idea of a smoke signal. A message was conveyed, but the place of that message had no ongoing sanctity. Indeed, those who received a message from God in this way were usually surprised by it. There was no expectation that another message would be delivered at the place where the metaphorical telegram reached its recipient. A good example of this first category was the burning bush in Exodus 3. When Moses approached the flaming shrubbery to see why it was

---

[15] Sara Japhet notes two of these categories in "Some Biblical Concepts." I have added a third category.

not consumed, God addressed him with a very specific command: "Remove your sandals, because the ground on which you are standing is sacred."[16] The revelatory presence of God turned regular ground into holy ground. However, after the revelation of God ended, there was no indication that the particular bush or patch of ground retained their special status.[17] The sanctity of the bush's locale resulted from the presence of God, and when that presence left, so did the need to give particular reverence to that spot.

The second subcategory is occupied solely by the tabernacle. This sacred place is roughly analogous to the earliest cell phones. All one needs to do is review a movie from the late 1980s or early 1990s to get an appropriate picture. Early "mobile" phones were big and unwieldy. They had long antennas that had to be extended to make a call, and they were impractical to carry around. And yet, they were an improvement in the range of communication that they allowed their owners to have. For the first time, the caller was not limited to a pay phone or landline inside a building. However, because of their size and expense, most people did not have one. Those few who did certainly did not carry them around like a wallet or a set of keys.

In many ways, the tabernacle was similar for the Israelites. It enabled them to have contact with God without being dependent on "landlines." While the Israelites wandered in the wilderness before entering the Promised Land, the tabernacle allowed them to have regular contact with God. When they packed up and moved, they would pack up the tabernacle as well, so that their primary connection to God would go with them. Thus, by providing the tabernacle, God supplied the Israelites with portable sacred space. Like the burning bush, when the tabernacle was set up, the ground that it occupied became holy; when they decamped, the ground that it

---

[16] "For the ground upon which you are standing, it is holy ground." Author's translation.

[17] It should be noted that this epiphany took place at Mount Horeb, which is called the "Mountain of God" in the previous verses. However, Japhet states that this epithet is not necessarily an indicator that the area is sacred ("Some Biblical Concepts," 60).

had occupied lost its sanctity. In this sense, the sacredness of the location depended entirely on the structures and objects associated with it. *Amen!*

The third and final subcategory consists of those places that retained their sacredness over time. The analogy that best fits these sites is the phone booth or landline found in a permanent structure. Whenever someone wants to make a call, they have to assume that it can be received on a landline at the other end. With the right payment and number, a call can be made with the reasonable expectation that it will go through. These sites are the embodiment of Exod 20:24's definition: "You shall make an altar of earth for Me, and you shall sacrifice on it your burnt offerings and your peace offerings, your sheep and your oxen; in every place where I cause My name to be remembered, I will come to you and bless you." Jerusalem and Shiloh were prime examples of this category. Jerusalem, of course, achieved a permanent status that was unrivaled in the land of Israel. Unlike many of the other cult sites that came and went before it, Jerusalem's status as an access point to God only solidified over time. *Hallelujah!*

Shiloh was the site where the Israelites gathered during the conquest of the land of Canaan and, consequently, it was also one of the locations where the tabernacle stood. However, unlike some of the other places where the tabernacle had been stationed, Shiloh became an enduring sacred place; by the period of the judges, the house of God was said to reside there ("all the time that the house of God was at Shiloh," Judg 18:31). In fact, a more durable structure than the tent seems to have been established on the site; in 1 Sam 1:9 and 3:3, this site was called a "temple of the LORD," having both doorposts and doors. Here, the young Samuel was brought and dedicated to the service of the Lord (1 Sam 1:24); in Jeremiah's temple sermon (chapter 7), God referred to Shiloh as the place where he caused his name to dwell, which is reminiscent of the language of Exod 20:24 and Deut 12. Shiloh clearly had a link with the divine; God was accessible there for worship and sacrifice on a regular basis. In other words, Shiloh was a phone booth where calls could be made and received.

The example of Shiloh in Jeremiah 7 also demonstrates that God's relationship with a particular sacred space can change. By the time of the prophet, Shiloh had been destroyed. Jeremiah, relating the words of God to the inhabitants of Jerusalem, stated, "Therefore, I will do to the house which is called by My name, in which you trust, and to the place which I gave you and your fathers, as I did to Shiloh" (v. 14).

Thus, Jeremiah attributed to God the destruction of this sanctified place. Furthermore, Jeremiah equated Jerusalem with Shiloh regarding God's relationship with the sacred space. The fact that Shiloh was a sacred shrine where God had accepted worship and sacrifice was not questioned by the people. Nor was it questioned in the minds of Jeremiah's audience that this sacred space had been destroyed and would now be unusable for worship. The prophet used these points to illustrate that Shiloh, once a sacred place, had fallen out of favor with God. Jeremiah insinuated that Jerusalem enjoyed no more of God's favor, security, or protection than Shiloh did. God's relationship with a place could and did change, and with it, the ability to communicate with God also changed. The phone booth had been disconnected and removed. JESUS!

So, O my ABBA,
Please, in the Name
of JESUS Christ,
Keep me forever
Connected with
Thee !
Love, Jo Johnson

CHAPTER 2

"WHEREVER I REVEAL MYSELF"

Defining Sacred Space in the Hebrew Bible

Introduction

Before we look at specific sacred spaces, it will be helpful to look at some foundational ideas about sacred space in the biblical text. We will focus on three primary texts that illustrate these ideas: Exod 20:24, Deuteronomy 12, and 1 Kgs 8:1–9:9. The Exodus passage sets the stage for worship at multiple sites, the Deuteronomy passage finds God asserting his right to establish sacred spaces according to his sovereign choice, and the 1 Kings passage focuses on the Jerusalem temple. These examples show the means and circumstances whereby God establishes his sacred spaces, and thus we turn to a careful analysis of them.

Foundational Texts, Foundational Ideas

Exodus 20:24

In Exodus 20, the people had just received part of the revelation of God at Sinai, including the Ten Commandments. God's presence blocked the people

from touching the mountain and being struck down (Exod 19:18–24). After
witnessing God's manifestation on Mount Sinai, the people were afraid. God
told them they were not to be frightened of him as a person, but of his judgment if they sinned (Exod 20:20). However, there was an implicit problem in
the fear of the people. It was the same problem that Adam and Eve had when
they hid from God. How would the people be able to communicate with God
on a regular basis, given what they had just witnessed at Sinai? *Good question!*

In verse 24, God addressed this concern by promising a means of communication at places he would choose. The verse reads: "You shall make an
altar of earth for Me, and you shall sacrifice on it your burnt offerings and
your peace offerings, your sheep and your oxen; in every place where I cause
My name to be remembered, I will come to you and bless you." Thus, God
would make himself available, and worship could take place.

The modern reader must keep in mind that as the people were leaving Mt. Sinai, they might have been concerned they were also leaving God
behind.[1] Their primary experience with the gods of Egypt would probably
have made them think their God was limited to certain places. However,
verse 24 offers reassurance that any such belief was mistaken. God would
come to them. He was not tied to Mt. Sinai or any other place. Thus, verse
24 serves, in part, as an affirmation of God's omnipresence, but more specifically, it indicates God could be present anywhere he wanted.[2] *Amen!*

Turning to the content of the verse itself, the Hebrew word usually
translated as "to remember" is crucial for understanding how a place came
to be sacred. In this context, the verb has a causative sense, with God as the
subject and his name as the object. So, God was the one who chose a site and

---

[1] Umberto Cassuto, *A Commentary on the Book of Exodus*, trans. Israel
Abrahams (repr., Jerusalem: Magnes Press, 1997), 256–257. The Hebrew term
for remember may also include the idea of invoking or calling upon in the Hifil
stem. I am grateful to Dr. Richard Sarason for this helpful reminder.

[2] "Omnipresence" is here defined in terms of God's relationship to particular
places, as opposed to the broader theological definition that states that God is everywhere simultaneously. See J. Kenneth Kuntz, *The Self-Revelation of God* (Philadelphia:
Westminster, 1967), particularly the section on theophany and the patriarchs.

subsequently made it holy. Umberto Cassuto suggests that a better translation than "where I cause my name to be remembered" would be "wherever I
reveal myself." This translation reinforces the idea that a sacred place was one
in which God made himself accessible. The manifestation of the divine presence would indicate to the worshiper that God was present and accepting of
sacrificial worship there.[3] God's revelation would mark a place as having a
phone booth, and he was able to put one anywhere he wanted.

Even in our own culture, someone's name can be a proxy for the person
himself. We complain about "getting our good name back" or about having
our names "dragged through the mud." We want to put our names on prod-
ucts that meet our standards and not on ones that fail to do so. Likewise, in
the ancient Near East, a person's name did more than serve as a handle to get
his attention. It represented that person and might even describe his unique
nature or vocation. Abraham, Isaac, and Jacob are three familiar examples.
But even more so, we have the case of Yahweh, whose name went before him
and which, for that reason, he guarded with special care and commands.
The God of Israel reveals himself as YHWH in Exod 3:13–15 and gives his
name to Moses with greatest solemnity. Therefore, when YHWH promises
that he will cause his name to be remembered in certain places, he does
more than promise the recollection of the sound 'YHWH.' He means that
he himself will be remembered and worshiped in that place.

In the Bible, God's name was synonymous with his acts and power
(cf. Exod 3:15; 9:16; 23:21; Num 6:27). Likewise, for God's name to have
been in a place or associated with a people showed that God was linked
to that place or people (1 Kgs 8:16, 29; 9:3; 11:36; 2 Chr 7:14, 16; Neh
1:9). Additionally, the name of God was to be treated with the same respect
due to God himself (Isa 42:8; 48:9; Jer 7:10; 44:26; Ezek 20:9, 14, 22, 44;
36:23; Mal 1:6, 11; 4:2).

---

[3] Levine notes that the Israelites believed that God was present at such a
site in the sense of being attuned to the place, rather than being continually
present or dwelling there. See Baruch A. Levine, "On the Presence of God in
Biblical Religion," in *Religions in Antiquity: Essays in Memory of Erwin Ramsdell
Goodenough*, ed. J. Neusner (Leiden: Brill, 1968), 79.

Yet the question remains: where would God cause his name to be remembered?[4] Was the idea in Exod 20:24 many different places, or was it more the notion of God being everywhere? The primary subject of the verse can be our guide here. The verse deals with building an altar. A single altar at a singular location does not make sense in the context of the instructions given. The verse states that the altar would be built in "every" place. The word in question can also be translated as "each" in this context. The people did not have just one stop in front of them, and in the Promised Land they would be spread out geographically. On the other hand, the verse seems to indicate that random selection of places *by the people* was prohibited. Instead, *God* would indicate the place via his self-revelation. Thus, the verse refers to select places where God would reveal himself.[5] Indeed, in verse 22, God reminded the Israelites that he had spoken to them from the heavens at earlier times. These conversations took place at particular places. Thus, God would continue to reveal himself to the Israelites on their journey, and the locations of these revelations would be acceptable sites for altar building and, consequently, sacrificial worship.

Once the site was acknowledged with the building of an altar and the offering of sacrifices, the verse states, "I [God] will come to you and bless you."[6] The idea of God coming to the worshiper(s) pointed to God's freedom in choosing sacred places. Even those places where God "causes his name to be remembered" cannot be thought of as a permanent abode for

---

[4] The phrase בכל־המקום is problematic in that the word כל can be translated as "every, any, each," or "all."

[5] However, Cassuto argues that this phrase, coupled with the fact that altar is mentioned only in the singular, has a centralized cult in mind, much like the passages from Deuteronomy. Cassuto, *A Commentary on the Book of Exodus,*256.

[6] As to God blessing the Israelites, this phrase most likely refers to gifts of fertility, respect, and wealth. Josef Scharbert notes, "Except for the tribal fathers whom Yahweh blesses out of pure grace, it is always assumed or (as in the case of Ex. 20:24 and Deut.) demanded that the person being blessed or Israel deserves the blessing because of fidelity to Yahweh and his law" (*Theological Dictionary of the Old Testament*, ed., G. Johannes Botterwick and Helmer Ringgren, trans. John T. Willis [Grand Rapids: Eerdmans, 1975], s.v. "ברך," 294).

him. In fact, the coming of God should be understood in the context of the preceding verses, in which God was present in the "thick cloud," but related to the people as one who had spoken with them "from heaven." Thus, Exod 20:24 is a statement of God's appearance at particular places on the earth, while at the same time, being an affirmation of God's freedom to choose those places. God's sovereign freedom with regard to sacred places is a prominent theme in Deuteronomy 12 as well. Accordingly, we will now turn our attention to that chapter.

Deuteronomy 12

The book of Deuteronomy is a long address to the nation of Israel as they were about to enter the Promised Land. Moses was soon to die, so he gave the Israelites a refresher course on how they should live in the land. This long speech assumes that the goal of life in the land of Canaan was to live life in fellowship with God. The land that Israel was about to enter was a place much like the garden of Eden, because they would have regular access to God. The book follows the form of a covenant treaty that was common in the ancient Near East to show the contractual obligations of this relationship.[7] Chapter 12 introduces how the Israelites were to worship God in the land and the nature of the places where this worship would take place.

Turning to the content of chapter 12, we find that the phrase "the place which the LORD will choose to make his name dwell there," is repeated three times with only minor variations (vv. 5, 11, 14). What exactly does it mean that a "name will dwell" at a place? In the context of Deuteronomy 12, the idiom emphasizes that Yahweh, the sovereign king, had claimed the land as his own. In other words, God would set up phone booths, so that the people could have regular contact with him. Given this meaning, what else does Deuteronomy 12 reveal about God's relationship to the Promised Land?

---

[7] See Meredith G. Kline, *Treaty of the Great King: The Covenant Structure of Deuteronomy: Studies and Commentary* (Grand Rapids: Eerdmans, 1963) and Peter C. Craigie, *The Book of Deuteronomy* (Grand Rapids: Eerdmans, 1976).

The instructions in verses 2–4 set the stage for the rest of the chapter.
The verses read,

> You must destroy all the sites at which the nations you are to dis-
> possess worshiped their gods, whether on lofty mountains and on
> hills or under any luxuriant tree. Tear down their altars, smash their
> pillars, put their sacred posts to the fire, and cut down the images of
> their gods, obliterating their name from that site. Do not worship
> the LORD your God in like manner.[8]

The first instruction related to worship at sacred places is a command to
destroy any objects and places that were sacred to any other deity. Peter
Craigie notes, "These objects were to be systematically destroyed so that
the places associated with them would be divested of any semblance of
sanctity."[9] Even as many of the inhabitants of the land of Canaan were to be
destroyed, so too were their sacred places and styles of worship.

The fact that the list is so specific concerning geographic markers
("whether on lofty mountains and on hills or under any luxuriant tree") is
telling. Those geographic features that formed some link to the Canaanite
gods were not to be associated with the God of Israel. Generally speaking, ancient Near Eastern religions found links to their gods in natural
phenomena, because the powers of the gods were evident in the elements
of nature. For example, Utu, who was represented by a flaming sun disk,
was the Mesopotamian sun god. Nanna was the moon god, and Ezinu was
the god of grain. Baal was associated with storms, so hills struck by light-
ning would be connected to him.[10] In our modern analogy, Canaanites

---

[8] Translation from *JPS Tanakh*, 1985. Verse 5 represented an ideological
break in the text, since it presented the alternative (adversative relationship) to
what vv. 2–4 described. Grammatically, the adversative was an opposite but parallel structure, so there should be no break here in relation to the overall narrative.

[9] Craigie, *Book of Deuteronomy*, 216. The connection between destruction
and de-sanctification will be explored in a later chapter.

[10] For more on this idea, see Thorkild Jacobsen, "Formative Tendencies in
Mesopotamian Religion," in *Toward an Image of Tammuz and Other Essays in*

thought that they would probably get better phone reception at the top of a hill than in a valley. By contrast, Deut 12:2–4 makes it clear that God could not be located via natural or geographic markers. Thus, worshiping at such places was not permissible for Israel. The God of Israel was not limited by geographic features; indeed, he created all of them and stood apart from them. This prohibition served, therefore, to assert the theological idea of God's transcendence; he was not limited like the pagan gods of the Canaanites.

Of course, the instructions of Deuteronomy 12 went beyond this ban on associating Yahweh with elements in nature. The text calls for an out-and-out destruction of all the Canaanite sacred places. Craigie maintains that this amounted to a symbolic act of rejection.[11] However, while rejection of the pagan worship sites was involved, the ultimate goal was more severe than just a symbolic rejection. The text states that the names of the Canaanite deities were to be obliterated from the cultic sites. A. D. H. Mayes notes that what was not named had no existence.[12] Ultimately, Yahweh was to be the only name that was called upon in the land of the Israelites. When God claimed the land by making his name dwell there, he also obliterated the existence and reality of other deities. Thus, the Israelites could not predict or pinpoint the place or places where God would make his presence known. J. G. McConville states, "The paradox is this: Yahweh enters a relationship with a people, Israel, which requires an actual location in space and time; yet Yahweh is not bound by any necessity to that people, nor to any place."[13] Not only were the Israelites to remove all traces of Canaanite worship, but they also could not identify sacred space by

---

Mesopotamian History and Culture, ed. William L. Moran (Cambridge: Harvard University Press, 1970). Jacobsen is heavily influenced by Rudolf Otto and his ideas about the numinous (*The Idea of the Holy*).

[11] Craigie, *Book of Deuteronomy,* 216.

[12] Craigie, 223.

[13] J. G. McConville and J. G. Millar, *Time and Place in Deuteronomy,* Journal for the Study of the Old Testament Supplement 179 (Sheffield: Sheffield Academic Press, 1994), 137.

naturally occurring symbols or geographic features. In this sense, the phone booths are dedicated lines. One could not use a Baal phone booth to call the God of Israel.

A second reason God warned against using such sites for his worship was that the acts involved in the worship of the pagan deities were detestable to him. Thus, verse 31 states, "You shall not act thus toward the LORD your God, for they perform for their gods every abhorrent act that the LORD detests; they even offer up their sons and daughters in fire to their gods."[14] In other words, Canaanite worship was wholly abhorrent to Yahweh, with the culmination of such detestable worship being the burning of children as a sacrifice. Such acts of worship were unacceptable, and would desecrate any place where they were carried out.[15] Richard Clifford notes, "An important de-sacralization takes place in these verses. Not every natural movement or act is automatically sacred, but only those declared so by the Lord."[16] Indeed, God refused to be associated with places where such detestable acts had occurred.[17]

The idea of God's choice represents the main thrust of the rest of the chapter. The choice of self-disclosure of Yahweh stood as a stark contrast to the Canaanite sanctuaries and any natural phenomena usually associated with the divine realm. In verses 5, 11, 13–14, 18, 21, and 26, the phrase, "the place which the LORD your God shall choose" is repeated with only slight variation. Verse 5 states, "But you shall seek the LORD at the place which the LORD your God will choose from all your tribes, to establish His name there for His dwelling, and there you shall come." This "place"

---

[14] Translation from *JPS Tanakh*, 1985.

[15] The issue of de-sanctification will be dealt with more fully in the following chapters.

[16] Richard Clifford, *Deuteronomy: With an Excursus on Covenant and Law*, ed. Carroll Stuhlmueller and Martin McNamara (Wilmington, DE: Michael Glazier, 1982), 78.

[17] The acts done at the sacred place can be compared to a phone number. One cannot dial God using the phone number of child sacrifice. I am indebted to Rustin Umstattd for this anecdote.

that the Lord would choose stood in direct contrast with the "places" of the Canaanites. Yahweh's choice is the focus of the verse, rather than the theoretical number of places allowed for worship.[18] The place "which the LORD your God will choose" remains unnamed, and the emphasis therefore remains on God's choice.

In summary, Deuteronomy chapter 12 delineates an important idea about God's relationship to sacred space. Sacred space, or more specifically, those places that had a connection to God (thereby making them acceptable places where God could be contacted and worshiped), had to be revealed by God himself. This is presented in the chapter first negatively and then positively. First, the prohibition against the Canaanite sacred places points to the fact that God was not tied to natural phenomena. Second, the chapter emphasizes that God would be the one to choose the acceptable contact points for worship. God's choice points to a dependence on him that ties into the covenantal or contractual nature of the book of Deuteronomy. God would provide phone booths for communication. The Israelites had no control over where God set up these points of contact. The only thing that they could know for sure was that the phone booths would not be located at the pagan places of worship. God would not communicate via pagan phone lines. New wires would be installed.[19]

---

[18] For some of the differing opinions and arguments, see A. D. H. Mays, *Deuteronomy* (Greenwood, SC: Attic Press, 1979); Craigie, *Book of Deuteronomy*; W. H. Irwin, "Le Sanctuaire Central Israélite Avant L'éstablissement de la Monarchie," in *Revue Biblique* 72 (1965): 161–84; Gordon J. Wenham, "Deuteronomy and the Central Sanctuary," *Tyndale Bulletin* 22 (1971): 102–18; John Van Seters, "The Pentateuch," in *The Hebrew Bible Today: An Introduction to Critical Issues*; Sandra L. Richter, *The Deuteronomistic History and the Name Theology* (New York: Walter de Gruyter, 2002); Jeffrey Niehaus, "The Central Sanctuary: Where and When?" *Tyndale Bulletin* 43, no. 1 (May 1992): 3–30; McConville and Millar, *Time and Place in Deuteronomy*; and A. Besters, "Le Sanctuaire Central dans Jud.," 19–21; *Ephemerides theologicae Lovanienses* 41 (1965): 20–41. On a fundamental level, the way one answers the question of Deuteronomy's authorship is determinative in this argument.

[19] I am grateful to Rustin Umstattd for this anecdote.

1 Kings 8:1–9:9

The third and final key passage is 1 Kgs 8:1–9:9, because it builds on the ideas about God's relationship to sacred places found in Deuteronomy 12. The setting for these verses is the completion of the temple. We see the placement of the ark of the covenant within the temple; God's presence moving into the temple, thereby sanctifying it; and a divine revelation to Solomon.

1 KINGS 8:3–13—MOVING OF THE ARK AND THE PRESENCE OF GOD

The first logical section of 1 Kings 8 that expresses ideas about God's relationship to sacred space is verses 3–13.[20] Within this section, a division can be made between the movement of the ark and the tent of meeting into the temple (vv. 3–9) and the presence of God filling the temple (vv. 10–13).[21] The sacrifices Solomon and the congregation of Israel offered before the ark (v. 5) point to their belief that God was in some way present or connected with the ark.[22]

As a result, the movement of the ark and the tabernacle into the temple showed that God was now associated with the new space of the temple. The placement of the ark under the wings of the cherubim was also a symbol of God's presence and connectedness to the new place, and found its inspiration in Exod 25:18–22. More specifically, in verse 22, God stated, "There I will meet with you; and from above the mercy seat, from between the two cherubim which are upon the ark of the testimony, I will speak to you about all that I will give you in commandment for the sons of Israel." God was regarded as enthroned upon the cherubim.[23] Thus, placing the ark under

---

[20] There is a longer parallel to 1 Kgs 8:1–13 in 2 Chr 5:2–6:11. Hurowitz considers the Chronicles account to be "midrashic." Victor Hurowitz, *I Have Built You an Exalted House,* Journal for the Study of the Old Testament Supplement 115 (Sheffield, UK: JSOT Press, 1992), 107.

[21] "Tent of meeting" is often cited as a vocabulary marker for a priestly redactor, but as noted above, this is unnecessary and overly simplistic. For example, see Gwilym H. Jones, *1 and 2 Kings,* New Century Bible Commentary, ed. Ronald E. Clements (Grand Rapids: Eerdmans, 1984), 194.

[22] The tabernacle as sacred space will be detailed below.

[23] See Jones, *1 and 2 Kings,* 192. See 1 Sam 4:4; 2 Sam 6:2; 2 Kgs 19:15.

the wings of the cherubim in the temple reinforced the idea that God was connected to the ark, and that he was reachable there. The space around the ark was always sanctified, whether in the tabernacle or the temple, because God had agreed to reveal himself between the cherubim.

However, the ark and cherubim would have been mere symbols without God's self-revelation that confirmed his presence was indeed in the temple. Verses 10–13 state that when the priests were leaving the inner sanctum, a cloud filled the "house of the LORD."[24] This "cloud" is clearly a reference to Exod 40:34–35, in which the tabernacle was covered by a cloud just prior to the manifestation of the glory of Yahweh.[25] The parallel is striking, for even as Moses was unable to enter the tabernacle because of the cloud and God's glory (v. 35), so too were the priests unable to enter the temple. The author of 1 Kings 8 might have been going so far as to imply that the temple was the nonmovable equivalent and successor to the tabernacle, since the elements of the tabernacle were being absorbed into the temple.

In verses 12–13, Solomon responded to the manifestation of the cloud in the temple.[26] He stated, "The LORD has said that He would dwell in the

---

[24] The infinitive construct is used to describe the leaving of the priests. Thus, the exact time relationship between their departure and the filling of the temple with the cloud is unclear. "With the infinitive construct, ב denotes in general the temporal proximity of one event to another." Bruce K. Waltke and Michael P. O'Conner, *An Introduction to Biblical Hebrew Syntax* (University Park, PA: Eisenbrauns, an imprint of Penn State University Press, 1990), 604.

[25] Simon DeVries feels that the term "cloud" here is a surrogate term for an original "glory of Yahweh." Simon J. DeVries, *1 Kings*, Word Biblical Commentary 12, ed. David A. Hubbard and Glenn W. Barker (Dallas: Word Books, 1985), 124–25. However, this falsely separates the cloud from God's glory. As in Exodus, the cloud is here depicted as covering or housing the actual glory of Yahweh. Therefore, the cloud is part of the whole and not a separate or surrogate means of description.

[26] Based on the witness of the LXX, there seems to be confusion surrounding these two verses. The LXX transposes the entirety of the verses after 8:53 and has a number of additions to the text. In v. 12, after "Then Solomon said," the LXX adds an explicative, "concerning the temple when he finished building it." Likewise, after "Yahweh" in v. 12, the LXX adds "has set the sun in the heavens," thereby creating a contrast with God's dwelling "in the dark cloud" (בעפרל). This

thick cloud." The cloud was not God himself; instead, it cloaked his true glory. In a very real sense, the cloud was depicted as a dwelling for God. A striking contrast arises here between Solomon's statement and the fact that he had built an actual house for God. The implication may very well be that the house was meant to be a replacement for the cloud. While it is difficult to clarify the nuance of "forever" at the end of verse 13 with any degree of certainty, it does stand in contrast to the former movement associated with the ark and the cloud that housed God's glory. With the movement of the ark into the temple, its journey was at an end, and it could, barring covenantal breach, remain in its new "house" forever. Likewise, the cloud containing God's glory had a permanent resting spot. This permanent spot is the equivalent of a home with a landline for communication. This is closer to resembling the garden of Eden than anything since the fall.

1 Kings 8:14–21—God's Choice

Verse 14 serves as a transition to Solomon's second speech (vv. 15–21). Within this passage, only a couple of ideas relate specifically to our discussion. First, verse 14 relates, "Then the king faced about." Some commentators believe this action was a response to the filling of the temple with God's glory. For example, Simon DeVries states that this was the natural response to the *mysterium tremendum* of Yahweh's glory.[27] Yet, the fact that Solomon

---

addition seems to restore the poetic balance to what is most likely a line from an ancient hymn, and thus, many translators include it in their translations. At the end of v. 13 of the MT, the LXX adds the phrase, "Is it not written in the book of the Song?" Most translators see this last addition as original and therefore as having dropped out of the MT. Some propose הישר for השיר rendering "song" as "upright one" (see Josh 10:12–13 and 2 Sam 1:17–27). Additionally, the LXX seems to have a corruption of the infinitive absolute בנה in v. 13, reading it as בתי which renders "I have built my house" instead of "I have surely built." In keeping with our method, we will follow the MT here, although there is merit to the addition of the phrase "has set the sun in the heavens." See DeVries, *1 Kings*, for a fuller discussion on the textual differences between the MT and the LXX.

[27] DeVries, *1 Kings*, 125. The term *mysterium tremendum* actually derives from Rudolf Otto's discussion of the natural response of a mortal to any encounter

made a prayerful statement prior to turning around makes it difficult to justify that interpretation. It is more likely that Solomon turned to face the people simply to bless them.

The next relevant verse in the section is verse 16: "Since the day that I brought My people Israel from Egypt, I did not choose a city out of all the tribes of Israel in which to build a house that My name might be there, but I chose David to be over My people Israel." The emphasis in this verse on God's choice is a clear echo of the theology of Deuteronomy—chapter 12 in particular. The language, on the other hand, reflects 2 Sam 7:6–7: "For I have not dwelt in a house since the day I brought up the sons of Israel from Egypt, even to this day; but I have been moving about in a tent, even in a tabernacle. Wherever I have gone with all the sons of Israel, did I speak a word with one of the tribes of Israel, which I commanded to shepherd My people Israel, saying, 'Why have you not built Me a house of cedar?'" Thus, verse 16 is a self-conscious reference to the Samuel passage.[28]

In both passages, the emphasis is on God's self-will. While 2 Sam 7:6–7 focuses on God's choice to move with the people of Israel through a connectedness with the tabernacle, 1 Kgs 8:16 focuses on God's connection with the person of David. Mordechai Cogan has aptly pointed out that Yahweh's delay in choosing a particular place for a temple should not be equated with a rejection of permanent habitation.[29] Rather, what God rejected was any control that mankind might have over determining where and when a temple could be built.

We must also briefly visit the phrase "that my name might be there" and the similar idea in verse 20: "the house for the name of the LORD, God of Israel." J. Robinson states, "Names were believed both to reveal and express

---

with the divine in his foundational study, *The Idea of the Holy* (London: Oxford University Press, 1923).

[28] See also 2 Chr 6:6, which is more explicit about Jerusalem.

[29] Mordechai Cogan, *1 Kings: A New Translation with Introduction and Commentary*, Anchor Bible Commentary (New Haven, CT: Yale University Press, 2001), 282.

character, so where God's Name was there he dwelt."[30] Thus, God was present at the temple. However, as in the case of God's "name" in Deuteronomy 12, Sandra Richter has, by comparing similar phrases in Akkadian, determined that, in most cases, actual presence is not intended. First Kings 8 is no exception. Richter states,

> This dedicatory prayer makes it clear that the *bayit* [house] built by Solomon is the ultimate symbol of YHWH's past and present relationship with his people—a symbol which serves to memorialize and perpetuate YHWH's acts of redemption in the midst of Israel and the nations. . . . It is also clear that the majority of idioms used in this text have nothing to do with divine presence.[31]

Richter's assessment that the "name" at a place was a symbol of ownership rather than the presence of the deity is mostly correct.[32] Nevertheless, in this particular context, God had just revealed himself in this new temple, not only claiming it as his own, but thereby associating his real presence with it. It was understood that God did not live in the temple any more than he had lived in the tabernacle.[33] That a god did not actually live in his or her temple was true for the ancient Near East as a whole.[34] Rather, a temple rep-

---

[30] J. Robinson, *The First Book of Kings*, Cambridge Bible Commentaries on the Old Testament (Cambridge: Cambridge University Press, 1972), 100.

[31] Richter, *Deuteronomistic History*, 90.

[32] Richter draws this from ancient Near Eastern parallels wherein kings are said to place their name on conquered territory, but are not actually present most of the time. Richter wisely notes that each idiom has to be taken in context to determine its exact meaning. See the section on Deuteronomy 12 above for more on Richter's work.

[33] There is always a tension between the ideas of God's transcendence and immanence. However, these two ideas should not be construed as separate theologies.

[34] However, the Mesopotamian gods were understood to be dependent on the temple and cult. See David Weisberg, "A Neo-Babylonian Temple Report," *JAOS* 87 (1967): 8–12; A. Leo Oppenheim, "The Care and Feeding of the Gods," in *Ancient Mesopotamia: Portrait of a Dead Civilization* (Chicago: University of Chicago Press, 1977); Yehezkel Kaufmann, *The Religion of Israel from Its Beginnings*

resented an open line of communication with the deity—a space in which the worshiper could be reasonably sure that his message reached the god in question because the place was assumed to be an intersection between heaven and earth. In 1 Kings 8 and the preceding texts that we have examined, the emphasis remains on God's choice to reveal himself. Verse 16, then, contains acknowledgment that God chose and accepted the temple dedicated by Solomon. As a result, the temple was a guaranteed conduit of communication with God.

1 Kings 8:22–53—Solomon's Prayer and Ongoing Contact with God

We jump now to verses 22–53, in which Solomon utters his prayer.[35] This prayer is rich with ideas and imagery relating to God and his connection to earthly space. Verse 22 creates an image of God's relationship with the temple even before Solomon begins to speak: "Then Solomon stood before the altar of the LORD in the presence of all the assembly of Israel and spread out his hands toward heaven."

Solomon was standing in front of the altar of the temple, arguably in the presence of God on earth. On the other hand, Solomon spread his hands toward heaven, also the acknowledged dwelling of God. The two ideas of God in heaven and God on earth were not mutually exclusive in the Bible. In our estimation, the only tension for the author(s) of the passage was present in describing the magnitude of God. Therefore, God's presence at both the altar and the temple was taken for granted in the narrative of 1 Kings 8 as a whole. God's immanence, or interaction with the created

---

to the Babylonian Exile, trans. Moshe Greenberg (Chicago: University of Chicago Press, 1960). The gods were also understood as "lords of the manor" in relation to their temples and their environs. See Thorkild Jacobsen, *The Treasures of Darkness: A History of Mesopotamian Religion* (New Haven, CT: Yale University Press, 1976), 81–84.

[35] The interceding verses either do not have direct relevance to a discussion of God's relationship to sacred spaces or the ideas have already been dealt with above.

world, and transcendence, or God's wholly separate nature from the created world, were two sides of the same coin.

This idea of God's presence in both heaven and at a particular point on earth is further developed in verses 23 and 27. Verse 23 is a broad opening statement in Solomon's prayer that praises God's attributes: "O LORD, the God of Israel, there is no God like You in heaven above or on earth beneath, keeping covenant and showing loving kindness to Your servants who walk before You with all their heart."[36] Here God is declared as distinct from all other gods and in all domains, whether heaven or earth, by virtue of his attributes. Solomon's exaltation of God implicitly indicates that the God of Israel was sovereign, even in spaces that would be considered sacred to other deities.[37] This theme of God's incomparability and superiority is repeated throughout the Scriptures (cf. Exod 15:11; Deut 4:39; Josh 2:11; Ps 86:8). Thus, J. Robinson notes, "The loyal Israelite was always in practice a monotheist, even when he could in theory acknowledge the existence of other gods."[38]

This theme is picked up again in verse 27, perhaps one of the most discussed verses in the Bible, by virtue of its allusions to God's transcendence and omnipresence. It makes explicit that which is implied in verse 23: "But will God indeed dwell[39] on the earth? Behold, heaven and the highest heaven cannot contain You, how much less this house which I have built!"

The idea of God's freedom and boundless nature does not need to be viewed as a correction to God's association with a particular place. The

---

[36] See Jon D. Levenson, "From Temple to Synagogue: 1 Kings 8," in *Traditions in Transformation: Turning Points in Biblical Faith*, ed. Baruch Halpern and Jon D. Levenson (Winona Lake, IN: Eisenbrauns, 1981), 154, and following for a discussion on the unity of vv. 23-53.

[37] Ultimately, the statement is one of praise, and as such, it is difficult to assess how much, if any, hyperbole is at work in the assertion. Given the context of worship, the statement may be persuasive and pedagogical in nature, but it is unlikely that the proposition of God's incomparability is an exaggeration of the actual belief.

[38] Robinson, *First Book of Kings*, 101.

[39] The LXX and 2 Chr 6:18 add "with mankind" here. The addition is minimal as far as meaning.

verse shows an awareness of the problem of believing that God would dwell permanently in any one place. As J. Robinson notes, "God cannot be circumscribed, only approached."[40] On the other hand, as noted above, God's presence in heaven and at particular points on earth were not considered incompatible notions. Even in the pantheon of ancient Near Eastern gods, the idea that the highest god dwelled in heaven was a very old idea.[41]

The main thrust of verse 27 is very closely associated with that of Exod 20:24 and Deuteronomy 12—God's choice. J. Robinson notes, "God has accepted the limitation of an earthly dwelling place because human beings need to meet him in a particular place in order that they may become aware of his presence in every place."[42] Within the context of the gratitude that pervades Solomon's prayer, verse 27 expresses thankfulness that God had chosen to focus his attention and presence at the place known as the temple in Jerusalem. Victor P. Hamilton summarizes the issue:

> Solomon repudiates the idea that the temple is God's only dwelling place. . . . The notion of divine immanence (expressed by the verb *shakan*) cannot overwhelm the notion of divine transcendence, anymore than the reverse can happen. Yahweh's inaccessibility to human eyes guarantees his transcendence, but his everlasting residence ("a place for you to dwell in forever" [8:13b]) on this rock of Zion guarantees his proximity (Terrien 1978: 196), thus creating the oxymoronic concept of an out-of-sight Immanuel.[43]

---

[40] Robinson, *First Book of Kings*, 102.

[41] See James A. Montgomery, *A Critical and Exegetical Commentary on the Books of Kings*, The International Critical Commentary, ed. Henry Snyder Gehman (Edinburgh: T&T Clark, 1960), 193. He notes that the idea of a celestial abode for the highest deities is commonplace in Semitic religion and dates to very early periods. One such example would be "Baal-of-the-Heavens."

[42] Robinson, *First Book of Kings*, 103.

[43] Victor P. Hamilton, *Handbook on the Historical Books* (Grand Rapids: Baker Academic, 2001), 399.

In other words, God was not limited by the structure of the temple, yet he chose to limit himself for the sake of communication and fellowship with his fallen, limited creatures. Thus, verses 23 and 27 affirm the freedom of God when it comes to revealing his presence at any particular place. With this idea established, we see in the rest of the chapter that Solomon entreats God for continued connection, presence, and receptivity to the place of his temple in Jerusalem.

This entreaty to God is contained within verses 29–53, with verses 29–30 serving as an introduction. Verse 29 reads: ". . . that Your eyes may be open toward this house night and day, toward the place of which You have said, 'My name shall be there,' to listen to the prayer which Your servant shall pray toward this place."

This continuation of verse 28 is foundational for the material contained in verses 30–53, as well as for our discussion of sacred space. First, we note a couple of parallels. The link between the words *house* and *place* is significant. The Hebrew term translated "place" can often imply a sacred place.[44] Thus, "the sacred place" is a parallel to "the house," and points to the sanctity of "this house." In other words, the two terms *place* and *house* work together to show that the temple is sacred space.

The second parallel can be seen in the phrases "your eyes may be open . . . toward the place" and "Your servant shall pray toward this place." Both God and the one praying were focused on "this place," that is, the temple; the storyline shows the role of the sacred place as the line of communication between God and his people. This understanding of sacred space as a line of communication between God and man reinforces the view that there is no contradiction in the idea that God can be present in an ongoing way both in heaven and at a specific place on earth. These are not conflicting ideas, but complementary ones. God, while dwelling in heaven and not bound by any

---

[44] See Roland de Vaux, *Ancient Israel: Its Life and Institutions*, trans. John McHugh (Grand Rapids: Eerdmans, 1997), 291. The word has to be examined in its contextual setting to determine whether it has this specialized meaning or is being used in a more general sense.

particular place, was at the same time present in a specific way at particular location, to be accessible to his people.[45]

The phrase "My name shall be there, to listen to the prayer which Your servant shall pray toward this place" builds on this idea that God could be present on earth and in heaven simultaneously. The implications of this phrase in the context of verse 29 and the 1 Kings 8 passage as a whole bears closer scrutiny.[46] As in Exod 20:24, the promise of God's name dwelling at the temple site was idiomatic for God's special association with the place. God was actively and willfully associated with the temple; he chose it. Likewise, similar to the function of the "name" in Deuteronomy 12, the "name" here served to demonstrate God's sovereign association with the place. Much as a conquered territory had the name of the conquering king on it, so the temple would be known as the sovereign domain of the God of Israel.[47] Taken together, the ideas surrounding the presence of the "name" of God at the temple point to a guaranteed association of God with the temple. It is this very association that guaranteed that Israel and even foreigners who came to the temple would have a line of communication with God.

This line of communication is the central focus of the rest of Solomon's prayer. Verse 30 begins the theme that would be repeated again and again: "Listen to the supplication of Your servant and of Your people Israel, when they pray toward this place; hear in heaven Your dwelling place; hear and forgive." In this prayer, Solomon reiterates and clarifies the idea that the temple (here referred to as "this sacred place") was a contact point between heaven and earth. When prayers were addressed toward the sacred space of the temple, God was asked to respond from heaven. In our ongoing phone analogy, the temple—and sacred spaces in general—functioned as a sort of phone booth with an open line from earth to heaven. Simon DeVries has hit upon this idea

---

[45] Being cut off from one's god is consistently viewed as a truly desolate state in both the Hebrew Bible and the New Testament. See, for example, the taunts of Elijah to the Baal prophets in 1 Kgs 18:27 and the anguish of Jesus in Matt 27:46; Mark 15:34.

[46] See sections on Exod 20:24 and especially Deuteronomy 12 above.

[47] See Richter, *Deuteronomistic History*.

as well: "The purpose is that the temple may serve as a listening-post or sounding board, continually receptive to any prayer that may be directed toward it."[48]

God established his connection to the place in verse 29 with the description of his "eyes" being open to the place and his "name being there." Yet Solomon acknowledges that God's nature was such that, while he may be connected with a particular place, he was never bound to it, for his actual dwelling was in heaven. God's connection to a sacred place had the same criteria that gave the site sacred status in the first place: God's choice to reveal himself.

The idea that a supplicant could pray toward the temple with the assurance that God would hear and respond is revisited seven times in the passage (vv. 32, 34, 36, 39, 43, 45, 49), illustrating the prime importance of the theme of connection between God and man via the sacred space of the temple. There is an expanding distance in these seven requests for God to hear and respond to prayer. The first four instances take place within the land of Israel, with progression of distance from the actual altar and temple. The last three potential prayer scenarios take place outside the land of Israel, with one instance even including the prayer of a foreigner. Thus, in verse 43, we see that the ultimate purpose of sacred space was not limited to Israelites alone. God established phone lines so that all who wished to communicate with God were able to do so. At this point, though, they had to access God through the landline in the house of Israel.

The common denominator of all seven instances of prayer is they were all directed to the Jerusalem temple. Here we have the idea that, although the assured connection between heaven and earth was a particular location, communication could be directed toward that place from a distance and still be heard. In terms of our ongoing phone analogy, we could equate this with a long-distance call. The temple, then, functions as a switchboard or possibly a cell phone tower that relays the message on to God. Thus, the petitioner could direct his request across the miles and trust that God

---

[48] DeVries, *1 Kings,* 125. DeVries is speaking specifically of vv. 28–29 here, but the idea remains valid for v. 30 and beyond.

would still hear it.[49] While physical presence in the temple was not required for the Israelite or the foreigner to communicate with God, orientation toward the sacred place was.[50] This requirement most likely played a role in the later ideological development that viewed a given sacred place as the center of the world.[51]

1 KINGS 9:1–9—GOD'S RESPONSE

In this last section of the passage, we see a confirmation of all that has gone before. Verse 1 summarizes the events of chapter 8, and in verses 2–9, "*Then* the LORD appeared to Solomon a second time, as He had appeared to him at Gibeon."[52] This revelation took place sometime after the dedication of the temple, but the message was clearly connected to that event.

While the vision at Gibeon resulted in a gift to Solomon (1 Kgs 3:5), the vision at Jerusalem ended in a warning against worshiping other gods. In 9:7–8, God warned Solomon of the consequences that would follow such idolatry:

Then I will cut off Israel from the land which I have given them, and the house which I have consecrated for My name, I will cast

---

[49] This passage is specifically addressing communication with God through prayer. Sacrifice was another category of communication entirely and seemed to be limited to the temple. Delving into the relationship between sacrifice and sacred space is beyond the scope of this particular study and cannot be dealt with here.

[50] Cogan, *1 Kings*, 286. See Dan 6:11. We will see in the following chapters that the line of communication between the sacred place and various points on the earth is bi-directional so messages from the heavenly realm originated at a sacred place and moved out from there.

[51] This idea is developed more fully by Eliade in *The Sacred and the Profane*. However, Eliade studies the concept from a comparative religions approach, and caution must be used when applying the idea to the biblical material. The idea is developed more fully in the rabbinic literature with respect to Jerusalem. See Martin S. Jaffee, *Early Judaism* (Upper Saddle River, NJ: Prentice Hall, 1997), 92–124, 164–212.

[52] Italicized word is my own change to the NASB translation here. It reflects the consecutive meaning of the verb construction.

out of My sight. So Israel will become a proverb and a byword among all peoples. And this house will become a heap of ruins; everyone who passes by will be astonished and hiss and say, "Why has the LORD done thus to this land and to this house?"

If the sanctification of a space such as the temple indicated there was a guaranteed point of communication with God at that place, then the destruction of that space would be a loss of communication. The house that was sacred because of God's presence would lose that connection. In other words, God would no longer be accessible, and the temple would be de-sanctified. Furthermore, the people themselves would be removed from the site, resulting in a double loss of connection at the earthbound point for both God and Israel. Such a removal of the people reflected the original loss of Adam and Eve, when they are removed from the garden. We will revisit this idea in more detail in the subsequent chapters.

While God could sever communication, the destruction of a place and the people's removal were described as Israel's responsibility.[53] God was the only one who could sanctify a place, but he was not the only one who could de-sanctify a place. Israel did not know what might be revealed as a sacred space, yet she had everything to do with whether the space maintained that connection with him.[54] Of course, such a statement does not mean that God could be pushed away by any power of men. Rather, he had graciously provided for communication, but covenantal unfaithfulness on the part of his people would be sufficient justification to terminate that connection.

In conclusion, 1 Kgs 8:1–9:9 provides several concepts of sacred space that are closely related to Exod 20:24 and Deuteronomy 12. First of all, there is the emphasis on God's choice when it comes to sanctification of the temple. Even though Solomon built a house for God, that "house" had no claim to sanctity unless God *chose* to sanctify it by revealing his presence there. This confirmation took place in association with the ark's placement

---

[53] See Robinson, *First Book of Kings*, 115.

[54] The topic of de-sanctification will be dealt with more fully in chapter 5.

in the temple and God's revelation to Solomon after his prayer. Secondly, one of the primary functions of a sacred place was to be a line of communication with God. Once God had revealed himself at the temple, it was assumed that he would be especially accessible there. Yet, 1 Kings 8 is unique from the other two texts that we have examined, in that it is careful to qualify that God was not bound to the sacred place of the temple. God might have been present at the temple in such a way that it was constantly on his mind, but he could also have removed the site from his attention. This cautionary concept leads to the final observation: although the temple had become a sacred place through the revelation of God, it could also be de-sanctified. Even as God's special presence at a place made it sacred, so the removal of his presence from the place would make it profane. Ironically, while God sanctified the temple, it was the actions of Israel that would break the line of communication. We will examine the idea of de-sanctification further in chapter 5.

CHAPTER 3

SACRED SPACE

One-Time Revelations

We turn now to the first of the three categories of sacred spaces described in chapter 1.[1] If sacred space in the Bible is that space where God revealed himself, then the places in this first category were sacred only during the actual revelation; they had no lasting sacredness. Therefore, we will designate this first category "one-time revelations" to indicate its temporary status. In our ongoing analogy, these communications between God and mankind can be thought of as telegrams. A message came through, often in unexpected ways, but then was finished. We can further divide these one-time revelations into two groups: revelations that did not mention the name of the place, and those that did. We can treat the former more briefly, since they ultimately do not contribute to an understanding of sacred space in the Bible.

God's Revelations without Any Link to a Place

The revelations of God that carried no association with space are evident in several passages (see Gen 6:13; 7:1; 12:1–4; 15:1–21; 17:1–22; Exod

---

[1] These categories obviously have limits and are, on a conscious level, foreign to the biblical text. With this caveat in mind, categories are needed in order to make sense of the complex relationship between the divine and terrestrial places.

5:22–6:3), but a few brief examples will suffice. In Gen 12:1–4, God called Abraham, and he obeyed. In this instance, a location is given, but it serves only as background information. The communiqué from God is not presented as unusual or unexpected. Abraham was commanded to leave his homeland, and he did so. The place held no significance for further communication with God, since the location was to be left behind.

In Genesis 15, God came to Abraham in a vision, and the place of revelation was again insignificant. In fact, one has to go back to 14:17 to find any mention of a particular place.[2] Genesis 15 differs from the example above, since God's interaction went beyond simple directions. In 15:1, God allayed any fear that Abraham might have had at being addressed by God himself. From there, God's interaction moved from speech to covenant ratification in a dream-vision (15:12–21). The fact that the dream-vision confirmed the covenant leads us to expect construction of a memorial or altar at the location. However, the text does not record any such activity. The place was not named and apparently had no ongoing association with God. Perhaps the focus on the covenant was the reason for the total disregard of the place, or perhaps it was the nature of the covenant—an ongoing bond between Abraham and his descendants with God through various journeys—that prevented a focus on the place. It is impossible to be certain, but it is clear that the place of this revelation was unimportant for future communication with God.

Genesis 17:1–22 differs a bit; when God's conversation with Abraham was over, "Then God went up from Abraham."[3] God's departure suggests an end to communications at that spot—hence, he did not confer special status to it. The focus was on the telegram, rather than the place where it was received.

---

[2] The place "valley of Shaveh" (עמק שוה) or "King's Valley" (עמק המלך) is mentioned as the meeting place for Abraham and the king of Sodom. It is unclear whether Abraham was in the same place during God's revelation in ch. 15.

[3] 17:22 (my translation).

In Exod 5:22–6:8, Moses had one of his many conversations with the Lord. Interestingly, just prior to the beginning of this interaction, Moses "returned to the LORD," yet no account is given as to where he was returning.[4] For our purposes, the main point is that Moses simply talked to God, and that the revelation was not considered extraordinary; therefore, the place of the divine-human interaction, once again, carried little to no significance. Moses's interaction with God was unique: he was the exception (Num 12:5–8). He was able to speak with God face-to-face. Thus, God represented a category in and of himself, and the rules of interaction with God were different by this point in Scripture.[5]

These examples illustrate the idea that divine revelation was not always spatially significant. These one-time revelations tended to occur to individuals in transition—those with no ongoing ties to the places they inhabited at the time of revelation. We can definitively say God's communication did not always automatically result in the demarcation of a space as sacred.

Moses and the Burning Bush

We turn now to an examination of those spaces that became sacred during an instance of God's self-revelation, but did not retain their sanctity after the revelation ended.[6] In other words, these spaces were specifically denoted as sacred during the event, but the effect was temporary. Two examples will illustrate this category. The first, and perhaps most prominent, example of this category is the burning bush revelation in Exodus 3.

---

[4] The mountain of God cited in 4:27 is probably in mind here, but this reference is far removed contextually.

[5] Initially, the "normal" rules of interaction with God did apply to Moses; this will be explained below in the section on the burning bush.

[6] Jeffrey J. Niehaus, "Theophany," *New International Dictionary of Old Testament Theology and Exegesis*, ed. Willem A. VanGemeren (Grand Rapids: Zondervan, 2001), 5:124. Niehaus argues that a place was only ever sacred during a revelation, and that God's holiness, which imbues sanctity, did not linger after God "departed." However, this is too narrow an explanation. At the very least, his definition of God's "departure" needs to be qualified.

In this passage, God caught Moses's attention with the bush that was set aflame, but not consumed. The revelation at the burning bush led to an extended conversation between God and Moses that stretches into chapter 4. However, only the first six verses discuss place sanctity, so those verses will be our focus. The first verse of the passage raises issues of location and space: "Now Moses was pasturing the flock of Jethro his father-in-law, the priest of Midian; and he led the flock to the west side of the wilderness and came to Horeb, the mountain of God" (Exod 3:1).

The location of Horeb is unknown. Some identify it with Mount Sinai, understanding Horeb to be an alternate name for Sinai, while others contend that Horeb is a separate mountain.[7] Ultimately, John Durham is correct in his estimation that the passage is more concerned with theology than geography; hence, the location of the mountain is not preserved.[8]

The anticipation of the designation "mountain of God" comes to its first fruition in verse 2: "The angel of the LORD appeared to him in a blazing fire from the midst of a bush;[9] and he looked, and behold, the bush was burning with fire, yet the bush was not consumed." The "angel of the LORD" has been the subject of some discussion about his role in the revelation. The majority of scholars agree that his role was minimal. He was probably associated with the visible manifestation of the "flame of fire" through which God revealed himself. Quite often, in fact, a fluid interchange existed

---

[7] Nahum M. Sarna, ed., *JPS Torah Commentary: Exodus* (Skokie, IL: Varda Books, 2004), 12. Sarna points out that there was no reference to the wilderness of Horeb as there was to the wilderness of Sinai. See also Nahum M. Sarna, ed., *Exodus* (Skokie, IL: Varna Books, 2004), and Cassuto, *Book of Exodus*.

[8] John Durham, *Exodus*, Word Biblical Commentary 3 (Dallas: Word Books, 1987), 30. Durham's point is well made, but must be treated with some caution. While geography may not have been the main issue for the author here, theology would not have been considered separate from the physical world. The connection between the physical and spiritual realms was of tantamount importance.

[9] The "bush" (הסנה) is sometimes seen as a symbol of Sinai (סיני) on the basis of spelling, but this is difficult, since סנה is a legitimate word for bush. See Durham, *Exodus*, 31.

between the "angel of the LORD" and God himself.[10] The text of Exodus 3 does not mention the angel again; rather, the revelation became a direct interchange between God and Moses.

Fire was a common symbol for the presence of God in the biblical narratives. What marked this particular fire as unique and divine was the fact that it burned without consuming the bush. It was a fire that needed no fuel to sustain itself. This was what grabbed Moses's attention. Verses 3–6 read: "So Moses said, 'I must turn aside now and see this marvelous sight, why the bush is not burned up.'[11] When the LORD saw that he turned aside to look, God called to him from the midst of the bush and said, 'Moses, Moses!' And he said, 'Here I am.' Then He said, 'Do not come near here; remove your sandals from your feet, for the place on which you are standing is holy ground.' He said also, 'I am the God of your father, the God of Abraham, the God of Isaac, and the God of Jacob.' Then Moses hid his face, for he was afraid to look at God."

Once God captured Moses's attention, God revealed himself. While the revelation was primarily through the spoken word, God was localized in the fiery bush.[12] Moses's surprise reinforces the idea that he was unaware of any association between God and the mountain. In fact, he had to be informed

---

[10] See Durham, *Exodus*, 30–31. C. F. Keil gives an extended discussion on the nature of the "angel of Yahweh/Elohim" in Carl Friedrich Keil and Franz Delitzsch, *The Pentateuch,* Biblical Commentary on the Old Testament, vol. 2, trans. James Martin (Edinburgh: T&T Clark, 1864), 118.

[11] There is more than one way to understand the syntax here, but the implication remains the same: the bush burned, but was not burned up. See David Noel Freedman, "The Burning Bush," *Biblica* 50, no. 2 (1969): 245–46 for an analysis of the various syntactical possibilities.

[12] Much has been written on the burning bush. For further reading on the burning bush itself, see Freedman, "The Burning Bush," 245–46; John Baker, "Moses and the Burning Bush," *Expository Times* 76, no. 10 (July 1965): 307–8; William Oscar Emil Oesterley, "The Burning Bush," *Expository Times* 18, no. 11 (August 1907): 510–12; G. H. Skipwith, "The Burning Bush and the Garden of Eden: a Study in Comparative Mythology," *Jewish Quarterly Review* 10, no. 3 (April 1898): 489–502.

that he was in a sacred place: "It is holy ground" (אדמת־קדש הוא).[13] Although the idea of sacred space can be implied by the term המקום, it is explicitly stated in this passage. The sanctity was a result of the presence of God, localized in the bush.[14]

Moses was instructed to remove his sandals, because he was standing on sacred ground. Most commentators understand this to have been a sign of respect and reverence. The idea was to avoid tracking dirt and filth into a sacred space, and this has correlations in modern religions.[15] In addition to removing his sandals, Moses voluntarily hid his face. This, too, is treated as a sign of reverence, mixed with a fear of God, by most commentators. Mesopotamian literature reflects a natural terror on the part of any mortal who encountered the divine, and the biblical literature extends this to an assumption that an encounter with the God of Israel would result in death, except by a divine stay of sentence. It is difficult to know how early this idea came into the religion of Israel, but it is not stated that Moses feared for his life here. Nevertheless, Moses's reaction may have gone beyond simple fear and reverence, since his reaction came after God identified himself as the God of the patriarchs.

---

[13] Translation mine. With the exception of the sanctification of the Sabbath referred to in Gen 2:3, the first occurrence of the root קדש is here with reference to the burning bush and sacred space.

[14] See Judg 9:15, in which Israel was identified with a lowly bush (אטד) among majestic trees. Whether it is proper to apply this analogy here or not would depend on the date of the respective narratives. Such an examination is outside our discussion of the sanctity of space and must be dealt with elsewhere.

[15] Muslims remove their shoes before entering a holy place, as do the Samaritans. Yet, there may be more to this than mere respect in the biblical world-view. Treading on something with one's feet can sometimes indicate possession of a place (Josh 1:3), and a shoe can be symbolic of trading rights and land (Ruth 4:7). Thus, when the Lord cast his shoe over Edom, it may have been idiomatic of possession or sovereignty over that territory (Ps 60:8; 108:9). If this is the case, then the removal of shoes in a sacred place may also have been an acknowledgment of the total lack of claim to that space by virtue of its special relationship to God.

The fascinating aspect of this passage is the temporary nature of the sanctity of the bush and its environs. This is one of the few instances in the biblical text in which God directly revealed himself to a person and explicitly declared the place of the revelation to be sacred or holy. And yet, once the revelation was over, no further mention was made of the bush or its location. After an extended discussion with God, Moses simply left and returned to Midian (4:17–18) without marking the spot in any fashion. He made no effort to offer a sacrifice there or even to return to the bush.[16] While the nature of the revelation was remembered later, in Deut 33:16 (". . . and the favor of Him who dwelt in the burning bush"), the narrative let the location of the bush fade from existence. Even though Horeb was the "mountain of God" on the basis of this revelation, there was no effort to build an altar or sanctuary at the site of the bush.[17] In other words, while the general area of the mountain was remembered (in part because of a future role it would play), the exact location of the bush was not. The assumption of the biblical text is that the connection between God and the burning bush ended at the same time as God's talk with Moses did.[18] In

---

[16] This is true of the immediate environment of the burning bush, which was declared "holy ground." However, the nearby "mountain of God" was described as the place where Moses would bring the Israelites to worship when they left Egypt.

[17] There was another revelation that specifically took place at Horeb, cited in 1 Kgs 19:8–18. In that narrative, it was Elijah who experienced an encounter with God. As in the Exodus 3 passage, Elijah, like Moses, covers his face when he realizes he is interacting with God. There is room for debate about the nature of the theophany to Elijah. See Jeffrey Niehaus, "In the Wind of the Storm: Another Look at Genesis III 8," *VT* 44, no. 2 (April 1994): 263–67. See also J. Lust, "A Gentle Breeze or a Roaring Thunderous Sound? Elijah at Horeb: 1 Kings XIX 12," *VT* 25, no. 2 (January 1975): 110–15. Whatever the case may be, the theophany did not result in an expectation of an ongoing connection between God and Elijah at Horeb.

[18] One reason for this may be that the connection moved from the bush to the person of Moses. God responded to the queries of Moses, regardless of place, after this episode, so there was no need for a specific contact point. Therefore, in the case of Moses, we are dealing with a sanctified person; sacred space became redundant.

other words, the telegram had been delivered, and the message was more important than the place.

Manoah, His Wife, and the Angel of the Lord

In Judges 13, we have another revelation in which there was a clear encounter with God, and yet the place of the encounter retained no lasting significance. The focus was on the miraculous birth of Samson. The passage in question runs from verse 1 through verse 24, with verse 1 serving as a broad introduction to the state of affairs in Israel at the time of Samson's birth and the rest of the passage detailing the visit of the angel of the Lord to Samson's parents. We will touch only on the verses relevant to the topic of sacred space.

In Judges 13, a connection with God was established in the first half of verse 3: "Then the angel of the LORD appeared to the woman." Did the "angel of the LORD" make the place sacred? There was often a certain fluidity between the angel or messenger of God and God himself. As J. Kenneth Kuntz states, "Total Old Testament usage of the *mal'ak* demonstrates that in any given case the *mal'ak* and the deity may be kept separate, partially merged, or fully merged."[19] Kuntz is correct, and each use of מאלך־יהוה must be examined in context. In this particular story, Manoah ultimately came to understand this messenger as synonymous with God himself (13:22).

Initially, however, neither Manoah nor his wife comprehended the identity of the messenger.[20] This lack of clarity was apparent in her description in verse 6: "Then the woman came and told her husband, saying, 'A man of God came to me and his appearance was like the appearance of the angel of God, very awesome. And I did not ask him where he *came* from, nor did he tell me his name.'" The messenger clearly made an impression, since he was

---

[19] Kuntz, *Self-Revelation of God*, 131. See the distinction between the מלאך and God in Exodus 3 above.

[20] Manoah's wife was never identified by name, even though she received the initial revelation.

"very awesome" in appearance, and yet there was some uncertainty about his real nature. Both his origin and the location of his message were a mystery. We are left to assume that the site was Zorah, a small Israelite town on the north side of the Sorek Valley, a few miles north of Beth Shemesh, simply because this site was Manoah's home (v. 2).

In what was apparently a need for reassurance and clarification, Manoah prayed for a second visit (v. 8).[21] The prayer acknowledged the heavenly origin of the message, but revealed Manoah's view that the messenger remained distinct from God: "O Lord, please let the man of God whom You have sent come to us again . . ." Manoah called the messenger a "man" of God, as opposed to the "messenger" or "angel." Of course, this was in keeping with his wife's description in verse 6, but may very well have reflected their combined understanding that they were dealing with a divinely inspired prophet.

Verse 9 relates the granting of Manoah's request, and this time, the text gives us one small detail about the location of the revelation: "and the angel of God came again to the woman as she was sitting in the field, but Manoah her husband was not with her." Once again, Manoah's wife received the revelation, even though her husband made the request for a second visit. She was sitting in "the field" (v. 9). This phrasing (with the use of the definite article) suggests that the field belonged to Manoah. The messenger/angel apparently waited in this field while the woman fetched her husband.

After Manoah met the messenger and asked him a few questions, he expressed his desire to prepare a meal for him.[22] The messenger refused the

---

[21] Some have understood Manoah's desire to meet the messenger himself as motivated by insecurity and hurt feelings that the message was given to his wife instead of him. See, for example, Daniel I. Block, *Judges, Ruth: An Exegetical and Theological Exposition of Holy Scripture*, The New American Commentary 6 (Nashville: Broadman & Holman, 1999). If such an interpretation is correct, then the second appearance, which was once again initially to the wife, must have been an additional wound to Manoah's pride.

[22] Manoah's motivation for wanting to offer a meal to the stranger was most likely hospitality, but the narrative does not explicitly give us a motive. See Block, *Judges, Ruth*, 412, for a discussion of other possible motives governing Manoah's offer.

meal, but agreed to stay while Manoah offered a burnt offering to Yahweh
(v. 16).[23] At this point, the narrative explicitly states that Manoah remained
unaware that he was entertaining the מלאך (the angel of the Lord). The
substitution of a sacrifice to Yahweh for a meal did not enlighten Manoah
any further, because he proceeded to ask for the messenger's name, which he
was not given, much as Jacob did not receive the name of his wrestling part-
ner (Gen 32:30, Eng: 29). The reason given for the denial is that the name
is פלאי, a word that has been translated variously as "wonderful," "beyond
understanding," and "hidden."[24] The implication was that the name was
too much for mortal comprehension. Yet interestingly, Manoah showed no
reaction to this news. We must, then, assume that he remained unaware of
the messenger's true identity.

Verses 19–22 contain the clincher for the divine nature of the revelation to Manoah and his wife. Manoah made a burnt offering on a stone,
and the text states, "Then he was doing wondrous deeds while Manoah and
his wife were watching."[25] There is intentional ambiguity here. The repetition of the root פלא (wonderful), used early as the adjective of the messenger's name, was certainly deliberate. It could refer to the Lord, who was the
recipient of the sacrifice, or to the מלאך (messenger/angel), who was initially
a bystander. The ambiguity is actually meant to show the loss of distinction
between the two.

---

[23] The story of Gideon bears some similarities to this one. However, whereas
Manoah remained obtuse about the identity of the messenger, Gideon seemed
more aware of his guest's nature and, from the very beginning, offered a מנחה
instead of a meal. See Block, *Judges, Ruth,* 410, for a more in-depth analysis of the
similarities between Judges 6 and 13.

[24] NASB, NIV, and JPS, respectively. The root is often used with respect to
God's acts of judgment and salvation. See Exod 15:11; Isa 9:5 (Eng. 6); 25:1, Ps
77:12, 15; 78:12; 88:11, 13; 89:6. As such, it may here be a foreshadowing of
the role Samson would play as God's tool of judgment and salvation. D. I. Block
sees significance in the fact that the only other appearance of this adjective is in
Ps 139:6, where it describes the wondrous knowledge of God (see Block, *Judges,
Ruth,* 413).

[25] My translation.

Verses 20–22 confirm this intentional ambiguity between Yahweh and his messenger:

> For it came about when the flame went up from the altar toward heaven, that the angel of the LORD ascended in the flame of the altar. When Manoah and his wife saw *this*, they fell on their faces to the ground. Now the angel of the LORD did not appear to Manoah or his wife again. Then Manoah knew that he was the angel of the LORD. So Manoah said to his wife, "We will surely die, for we have seen God."

It is unclear whether the ascension of the מלאך־יהוה (angel of the Lord) was the reference of the earlier phrase ומפלא לעשׂות (performed wonders), or whether there were other "wondrous deeds" besides the ascension. Either way, the Danite couple finally realized that they were, in fact, experiencing a theophany—a manifestation of God himself—rather than interacting with a prophet. They fell to the ground in a posture of worship, and Manoah feared death for interacting with the holy God face-to-face.[26] Manoah was now making little distinction between Yahweh and the messenger/angel.

In the end, even though Manoah and his wife recognized the מלאך־יהוה (angel of the Lord) as a divine revelation and, subsequently, that they were flirting with mortal danger by being in his presence, the place of the revelation was in no way memorialized. At least two reasons can be given for this. First, the nature of the message—namely, the birth of a son and its encompassing stipulations—was such that there was no expectation of ongoing communication at the place of revelation. In fact, Manoah had to make an entreaty to God for the second encounter to occur. A second reason arises from the nature of the story. The narrative is not concerned with ongoing worship or contact with God. After all, verse 1 reminds the reader that Israel had once again done evil, resulting in her oppression. As far as the narrator

---

[26] In this fear, Manoah is portrayed as less than rational, because his wife had to reason with him that, if God were going to kill them for the preceding interaction, they would have already been dead (v. 23).

is concerned, a people in such a state were not seeking or expecting regular contact with God. Ultimately, while the place of revelation to Manoah and his wife bore the necessary criteria to constitute sacred space, its sanctity was short-lived and very limited in scope. Indeed, the holiness of the messenger went largely unnoticed during much of the actual revelation. Once again, the telegram served its purpose, and once the communication was finished, the site itself was left with no remaining special or sacred status.

Conclusions and Comparisons of Exodus 3 and Judges 13

Both Exodus 3 and Judges 13 recount a direct self-revelation of God. While only Exodus 3 overtly describes the sanctification of earthly space, Judges 13 implies the divine presence by the reaction of Manoah and his wife. In both cases, the place of revelation was given no particular reverence after the experience was over, because there was no expectation that there would be ongoing contact with God in that location.[27]

It is interesting to compare an aspect of Exod 20:24 with Judg 13:18. Exodus 20:24 states that wherever God caused his name to be remembered would be an acceptable place for ongoing worship.[28] As was noted above, the association of God's name with a place was a way of acknowledging a special connection with, and even ownership of, a place. In Judg 13:18, however, no name was given, and the place did not become a significant spot for worship. In Exodus 3, God did give his name before the end of the revelation, and yet the burning bush itself did not retain any long-term sanctity for worship.[29] Thus, the two passages only illustrate that not every place where

---

[27] With respect to Exodus 3, we refer specifically to the immediate environs of the bush, which were declared "holy ground" during the revelation to Moses and not to the more generalized locale of the "mountain of God," which would become significant for the people after the Exodus.

[28] "Or caused his name to be invoked"

[29] However, the nearby "mountain of God" was mentioned in v. 1, prior to the revelation, and God described it as the place to which the people would return for worship when they left Egypt (v. 12). Sara Japhet describes the burning bush

God revealed himself ended up being a continuing point of communication. Some places just happened to be the destination point of the telegram.

In summary, the revelation in Exodus 3, while temporarily sanctifying the area around the burning bush, was also the initiation of a special relationship between God and Moses that was not limited to one area. Thus, there was no need for Moses to return to the bush in order to communicate with heaven. The revelation in Judges, on the other hand, entailed an announcement with a time-bound framework. Whereas Moses required ongoing communication to accomplish his divinely appointed task, Manoah and his wife were given all needed instruction, and even that was repeated for them. In both cases, it was understood that there would be no ongoing communication with God at the site of revelation. In both passages, the sanctity of the place, which was derived from its association with God via his messenger, was limited to the time required for the particular message of the revelation. This idea has significance for our discussion of the de-sanctification of space below. More immediately, however, it has significance for another kind of sacred space, the tabernacle.

Sacred Space: The Tabernacle

The tabernacle occupies a unique position in any discussion of sacred space. There is a copious amount of secondary literature on the tabernacle, with a particular focus on its association with the ark of the covenant. One could write a volume tracing the history of research on the tabernacle and ark of the covenant alone. Of necessity, the amount of material on which we touch, both in the biblical material and secondary literature, will be limited. While the secondary literature on the tabernacle is extensive, very little of it focuses exclusively on the tabernacle in relation to sacred space. The biblical material assumes the sanctity of the tabernacle and is therefore limited in its

---

episode as "dynamic" rather than ongoing. She notes that the "mountain of God" was linked with God's revelation, but the idea of a cosmogonic mountain of the gods—where the gods actually dwelt—is fundamentally foreign to the Bible. See Japhet, "Some Biblical Concepts," 59–60.

explanation of this sacredness. Our main goal is to illustrate the particular role the tabernacle occupies in the biblical concepts of sacred space and communication with God.

The tabernacle's sanctity is assumed in the biblical text on the basis of its ongoing connection with the God of Israel. There are several passages that illustrate this idea (see Exod 40:21; Lev 15:31; Num 3:38; 5:17; 9:18), but one will suffice. Exodus 40:34–35 recounts how God entered the newly completed tabernacle: "Then the cloud covered the tent of meeting, and the glory of the LORD filled the tabernacle." Moses was not able to enter the tent of meeting because the cloud had settled on it, and the glory of the Lord filled the tabernacle.[30]

God's presence in the tabernacle was unmistakable. The Hebrew text uses the term מִשְׁכָּן for the tabernacle, which carries the idea of "to dwell." Additionally, the tabernacle functioned as a kind of "miniature Sinai," as seen in the way that God appeared there (Exod 19:9; Num 9:19).[31] Unlike some revelations, such as the burning bush, in which the revelation initially only piqued the curiosity of the observer, this display was intentionally awe-inspiring. There was no mistaking that God associated with this tabernacle that had been built for him. This manifestation of God would conspicuously remain in order to guide the Israelites in their wilderness journey and to provide a direct form of communication.[32] The latter idea is spelled out

---

[30] We have in this passage two of the three terms used for the structure, "tent of meeting" (אֹהֶל מוֹעֵד) and "tabernacle" (הַמִּשְׁכָּן). The third term, usually translated "sanctuary" (מִקְדָּשׁ), carries with it the specific idea of sanctity. See Exod 25:8, Lev 12:4, and Num 3:28. See Richard E. Averbeck, "miqdas," in *New International Dictionary of Old Testament Theology and Exegesis,* gen. ed. Willem A. VanGemeren (Grand Rapids: Zondervan, 2001), 2:1078–87.

[31] Cassuto, *Book of Exodus,* 484. The revelation at Sinai became an ongoing and moveable event via the tabernacle. See R. E. Averbeck, "tabernacle," in *Dictionary of the Old Testament Pentateuch,* ed. T. D. Alexander and D. W. Baker (Downers Grove, IL: InterVarsity Press, 2003), 807–27.

[32] The pillar of cloud by day and fire by night, which led the Israelites in association with the cloud filling the tabernacle, would indicate an ongoing connection, as opposed to a one-time event. See Cassuto, *Book of Exodus,* 485.

more clearly in Exod 25:22 and Num 7:89, which explain that God would speak to Moses from above the ark within the tabernacle.

The biblical text explains the tabernacle's space in terms of the rules for approaching the holy space and objects within. In Lev 15:31, for example, the Israelites were warned that anyone who approached the tabernacle in an impure state would die. Likewise, in Num 1:51, only the Levites were to assemble and disassemble the tabernacle; any non-Levite who attempted to handle the parts of the tabernacle would be put to death. Within the ranks of the Levites, Num 4:19–20 notes that only Aaron and his sons could look at the most holy things; any other Levites who went in and looked would die.[33] Even as Moses was required to take off his sandals when he was on holy ground, so strict regulations were set in place because of the sanctity of the tabernacle. The tabernacle was sacred space because God's presence was there. The tabernacle's space had strict boundaries, since it was in the middle of the Israelite camp (see Exod 25:8; 29:45).

As we move on to Exod 40:36–38, we see further clarification of what makes the tabernacle holy. The passage states,

> Throughout all their journeys, whenever the cloud was taken up from over the tabernacle, the sons of Israel would set out; but if the cloud was not taken up, then they did not set out until the day when it was taken up. For throughout all their journeys, the cloud of the LORD was on the tabernacle by day, and there was fire in it by night, in the sight of all the house of Israel.

The key element here is when the cloud—the manifestation of God—moved, the people of Israel and the tabernacle moved, too. The choice to

---

[33] Here we have the idea of degrees of holiness, with the level of sanctity decreasing as one moved further from the center of revelation. Ezekiel's idealized temple expressed this idea most fully, and the rabbis continued to develop it after the biblical period. Exploration of it beyond the scope of this project is developed more fully by Philip Peter Jensen in his work, *Graded Holiness: A Key to the Priestly Conception of the World,* JSOTS 106 (Sheffield, UK: Sheffield Academic Press, 1992).

move, and conversely, the choice of place in which to set up the tabernacle, belonged to God and not the people.[34] The place would become sacred by virtue of the presence of the tabernacle, or more precisely, the God who dwelled within it. An expansion of this idea can be found in Num 9:15–23. The people of Israel, with the tabernacle in their midst, moved only in accordance with the movement of the "cloud."

What is interesting about the moveable nature of the tabernacle is that, unlike other revelations, God did not associate with a particular piece of static land, but rather, with the objects of the tabernacle.[35] Numbers 3 and 4 illustrate this association with a list of responsibilities for tearing down and setting up the tabernacle. The various Levitical families were given very specific duties concerning the movement of the parts of the tabernacle. The specific boundaries were not to be crossed on pain of death. Nowhere was there a prohibition against trespassing on the space formerly occupied by the tabernacle, though. This silence is perfectly logical in light of the holiness ascribed to the components of the tabernacle. The space was only sacred as long as the tabernacle sat upon it.

Summary and Conclusions

In summary, there are two ideas at work with respect to the sanctity of the tabernacle. The first is the fact that the tabernacle was indeed sacred "ground." God revealed himself in the tabernacle, and this was an ongoing connection. Second, the divine connection was with the actual structural components and the enclosed airspace of the tabernacle, rather than with any piece of land. As a result, the sacred space of the tabernacle was transferable to a new piece of land. While the tabernacle was set up, the place it occupied was holy ground, but once it was packed and moved, the

---

[34] See Japhet, "Some Biblical Concepts," 63.

[35] Sara Japhet fails to mention this important point in her analysis of the tabernacle as sacred space. The sanctity did, in some manner, continue—just not with the place. See Japhet, 63.

sanctity went with it, and the ground lost its holy status. With the presence of the tabernacle and the ark of the covenant, God had effectively given the Israelites a cell phone. The means of communication between God and his people could move with them. However, God was the one who determined when and where that phone had access to service.

The tabernacle, as moveable sacred space, was truly a unique form of connection between the divine and terra firma. It differed from those sites that were connected to God only during the moment of revelation. In one sense, the tabernacle served as a transitional point of connection with God between the periods of the wilderness wanderings and the settlement of Canaan.[36] Once the tribes had settled down to a sedentary existence, the need for a moveable sacred space would diminish.[37] It was during the settlement that the more static points of contact with God gained importance; this will be the focus of our next chapter.

Ultimately, God's choice to reveal his presence remained paramount, even with the tabernacle and its movement. This is a conspicuous theme that runs through all the material examined so far, and it will continue to be prominent in the third category of sacred space: places with ongoing sanctity.

---

[36] This is, of course, from the view of history in the biblical corpus. It is problematic to talk of the ideas of any particular source, as we cannot know what was cut and what was used. We can only speak of the ideas of the current form of the text.

[37] A detailed analysis of the tabernacle as sacred space and its ultimate fate is beyond the scope of this book. The interested reader is encouraged to examine the work of Richard Elliott Friedman, "The Tabernacle in the Temple," *BA* 43 (1980): 241–48 and Victor Avigdor Hurowitz, "The Form and Fate of the Tabernacle: Reflections on a Recent Proposal," *JQR* 86, no. 1/2 (July–October 1995): 127–51.

CHAPTER 4

A STAIRWAY TO HEAVEN

Places with Ongoing Sanctity

Introduction

In Judges, a significant shift takes place—Israel's conquest and settlement of the Promised Land. The Israelites were no longer a nomadic people, roaming from place to place, but a people settling on the land, and this change was mirrored by a change in sacred spaces, from the temporary places of connection that we examined in the last chapter to sacred places with a greater sense of permanence (cf. Deut 12:8). Yet, many of the ideas found in the previous chapter carry over to the sacred places of the land of Israel. During this period, we see many examples of places that serve as long-term phone booths—places where God revealed himself and could be reached even after that initial revelation. Four of the clearest examples are Bethel, Beersheba, Gilgal, and Shiloh.

Bethel

Bethel was an important site in the lives of the patriarchs and during the conquest and settlement of the land. It also became very important for the northern kingdom of Israel when the country divided (1 Kgs 12:16–17). The most significant passage on its sanctity is Gen 28:10–22. It not only tells us how Bethel got its name, but also explains how it achieved its sacred status.

Genesis 28:11 states that Jacob came to a place (Heb.: מקום) and camped there, simply because the sun had set. Nothing else seemed to be affecting Jacob's decision. However, the author may be giving the reader a hint of the importance of the site in his choice of the word מקום (place), a term often associated with sacred places.[1] The repeated use of the word (vv. 11, 16, 17) indicates the sacred nature of the place, even though Jacob did not know about it at the time. Furthermore, it is curious that the author relates that Jacob used some of the stones for a headrest (28:11). This, too, may be a foreshadowing on the part of the narrator about the nature of the place, since stones were often set up as markers of important spots (Gen 28:22; 31:45; 35:14; Josh 4:5–7; 24:26–27).

Jacob soon realized that he had stumbled on a sacred area by virtue of his vision. The most fascinating aspect of the vision is the connection of the stair from earth to heaven. According to verse 12, "He had a dream, and behold, a ladder was set on the earth with its top reaching to heaven; and behold, the angels of God were ascending and descending on it." This connection was the essence of what defined a sacred place. It was a particular link between earth and God's heavenly realm; it was a phone booth between God and man, and calls could be placed and received at both ends. In our passage, Jacob received an unexpected incoming call that surprised him and

---

[1] See de Vaux, *Ancient Israel*, 291. De Vaux understands מקום to mean "a place of worship," and that the author is indicating Jacob recognized Bethel as such from the very beginning. However, this interpretation does not fit with the level of surprise with which Jacob reacted following his vision. See the *International Standard Bible Encyclopedia*, ed. Geoffrey W. Bromiley, rev. ed., 4 vols. (Grand Rapids: Eerdmans, 1988), s.v. "Bethel," for more on the use of מקום. Sarna believes that the sanctity of the site came through the vision, and that Bethel was not sacred prior to that vision. He states, "The sanctity of the site is understood as deriving solely from the patriarch's theophanic experience." Nahum M. Sarna, *Understanding Genesis* (New York: McGraw-Hill, 1966), 192.

opened his eyes to the fact that he had indeed stumbled on a divine connection point.[2]

In Jacob's dream, God promised to give the land that he was lying
on to him and his descendants. The wording here is significant. Verse 13
reads, "And behold, the LORD stood above it [the stairway] and said, 'I
am the LORD, the God of your father Abraham and the God of Isaac; the
land on which you lie, I will give it to you and to your descendants'" (Gen
28:13). The use of the term הארץ (the land) here, rather than the term
מקום (place) indicates a change of some kind. While מקום means "place"
or "sacred place," ארץ (land) is a broader term that refers to a wider area of
land than just the spot where Jacob was lying on the ground. Thus, God
was not just promising Jacob the specific parcel of land on which he was
experiencing the vision, but a wider territory. This shows that sacred places
were part of a larger plot of land.[3] In other words, sacred spaces did not
stand ethereally detached from the land around them. They remained part

---

[2] It is interesting to note the differences in translations concerning where
God was standing in the vision. The Jewish Publication Society translates the
preposition/suffix combination עליו as "beside him" (so Sarna, *Understanding
Genesis*, 191). The NIV translates it as "above it." The antecedent of the pronoun
is unclear. It could refer to the ladder or stairway if the pronoun is translated
as "above" or "upon"—both are acceptable options. If the pronoun is translated
"beside"—also an acceptable option—then Jacob may be the antecedent (see
Cornelis Houtman, "What Did Jacob See at Bethel?" *VT* 27 [1977]: 348). The
latter is also supported by the use of the verb *said* rather than *called*, as well as
Jacob's understanding that the "LORD is in this place." See Waltke, *Genesis, A
Commentary*, 391. John Walton makes a case for the translation "beside," but
understands the antecedent to be the staircase (John Walton, *The NIV Application
Commentary: Genesis* [Grand Rapids: Zondervan, 2001], 571). However, normal
spatial relationships may or may not apply to a dream narrative. Either way, the
fact that there is a link between this point on the earth and the heavenly realm is
clear. Indeed, the point of the stairway is that "heaven has come to be on earth"
(Walter Brueggemann, *Genesis: A Bible Commentary for Teaching and Preaching*
[Atlanta: John Knox Press, 1982], 244).

[3] If Ezekiel's vision of the glory of the Lord departing the temple in stages
(Ezekiel 9–10) is an indicator, then it can be said that sacred places extended a
certain sanctity to the territories in which they were found.

of the earth, while simultaneously maintaining a special status due to their link with God.

Jacob's exclamation upon awaking from his dream is telling.[4] In verses 16 and 17, he proclaimed, "'Surely the LORD is in this place, and I did not know it.' He was afraid and said, 'How awesome is this place! This is none other than the house of God, and this is the gate of heaven.'" This statement revealed two key truths. First of all, Jacob's immediate reaction referred to the place—not the dream, not the promise, not even the fact that he was singled out—just the place.[5] In Jacob's worldview, certain places had specific links to God, and Jacob did not believe that such a dream revelation could take place just anywhere. Secondly, it reveals that there were no distinguishing marks to indicate to Jacob that he was at a sacred place when he bedded down for the night; it was only God's revelation that indicated to him the special nature of the place. Once again, we see that the sacredness of the place was determined by the action (here: revelation) of God.

Jacob elaborated on his assessment that he was at the "house of God" with the phrase, וזה שער השמים ("and this is the gate of heaven"). At its most basic, a gate was an access point into an enclosed structure or city. So the gate of heaven would have been an access point into the divine realm that was otherwise blocked off. If we understand the phrase "and this is the gate of heaven" as a further clarification of the statement "this is none other than the house of God," we have a greater insight into the nature of a "house of God." For Jacob, the house of God was a gate to heaven. It was an

---

[4] Jacob's experience was truly a dream, since he seemed to have been passive through the episode and only reacted when he awoke.

[5] Sarna, *Understanding Genesis*, 193. Sarna notes that while Abraham and Isaac did not express surprise at divine revelations, the narrative highlights Jacob's astonished reaction. Even if there had been previous cultic activity there, Jacob seemed to be unaware of it. "The text is most emphatic about Jacob's ignorance of the holiness of the place. In fact, there was nothing there at all, only stones."

access point at which communication with the divine realm could be sent and received.[6]

The סֻלָּם ("stairway")[7] that Jacob saw, with angels ascending and descending on it, further clarifies the purpose of the sacred place. In the biblical, ancient Near Eastern, and, subsequently, rabbinic worldviews, angels or divine beings were often thought of as having a territory over which they watched. Thus, the angels in Jacob's dream may be understood as reporting to God and then going back out to their assignments.[8] This would have ultimately been a symbol of God's protection of Jacob. The angels would have been privy to God's instructions via the promise issued to Jacob in the dream. Jacob's wonder at having camped at such a place is understandable.

What Jacob did next underlines the fact that there was no significant structure at the site: "Jacob rose early in the morning, and took the stone that he had put under his head and set it up as a pillar and poured oil on

---

[6] There was no concept of God "dwelling" at the site at this point. In fact, God was located on the heavenly side of things in Jacob's dream. The place was a conduit to the heavenly realm. John Walton, in *NIV Application Commentary: Genesis*, 571, describes sacred space as a "portal" between the divine and earthly realms. This is the same idea associated with ziggurats, although the fact that God was standing next to the ladder in heaven sets this vision apart from the ancient Near Eastern idea of gods descending to the earth.

[7] Translated by various commentators as "ladder, stairway" or "ramp." The image conjured in the modern mind by the word *ladder* does not seem aesthetically appropriate here. The angels were coming and going as on a major traffic path. De Vaux prefers "stairway" or "ramp" and notes that it has a religious parallel to the ziggurats of Mesopotamia. The ziggurats seem to have had a sanctuary at both the top and bottom of the structure, symbolizing a connection between heaven and earth. The sanctuary at the top was either the dwelling place of the god or a resting place, whereas the sanctuary at the bottom was where the god appeared. See de Vaux, *Ancient Israel*, 281–82; Abram Smythe Palmer, *Jacob at Bethel: The Vision—the Stone—the Anointing: An Essay in Comparative Religion* (London: David Nutt, 1899), 31–38; Gerhard von Rad, *Genesis: A Commentary* (Philadelphia: Westminster Press, 1972), 284.

[8] The idea that angels had territories or assignments that they had to travel to is developed more in the apocalyptic literature of the Bible. See, for example, Daniel 10 and Zechariah 1:9–17.

its top" (28:18). By setting up the stone as a religious "pillar" and anointing it, Jacob provided a marker for the place. Interestingly, Jacob called the מצבה (pillar) the "house of God." He did not mean a literal structure here; instead, the term referred to the object or the site as a whole.[9] In other words, Jacob was making an effort to mark the site as sacred.[10] This would not only help Jacob find the site again, but would also serve as a marker for others who came that way. In addition to setting up the pillar (מצבה), Jacob named his campsite.[11]

The last verses of the passage focus on Jacob's vow, in which he certified the place to be a communication portal to God. Jacob swore that if the conditions of his vow were met—God's abiding presence, food, and safety—then he would worship God and give a tenth of what he had to him. Perhaps more importantly, Jacob indicated that Bethel would be the primary place for his worship of God. Whether he intended to build a more substantial structure for worship later on is unclear. What *is* clear is that Jacob viewed Bethel as his primary means of encountering God.

While Genesis 28 is the main story illustrating the sanctity of Bethel, its connection with God is confirmed elsewhere. For example, in Gen 31:11–13, Jacob relayed to Rachel and Leah a dream that he had, in which an angel from God gave him instructions. In the dream, God spoke through the angel and said, "I am the God of Bethel, where you anointed a pillar, where you made a vow to Me; now arise, leave this land, and return to the land

---

[9] While a מצבה could have various functions, such as a commemorative stele to an alliance (Gen 31:45, 51–52; Exod 24:4; Isa 19:19–20) or a monument in honor of the dead (Gen 35:20; 2 Sam 18:18), it had special significance in relation to worship sites.

[10] See Gordon Wenham, *Genesis 16–50*, Word Biblical Commentary 2 (Dallas: Word Books, 1994), 223.

[11] Jacob was no doubt calling his campsite "Beth-El," not the city west of the site that carried the name Luz. I am indebted to Dr. Richard Sarason for noting that in Genesis 12:8, the city of Bethel was also west of Abraham's altar. The city of Luz would eventually come to be called Bethel in association with the sacred site near it. Jacob's camping spot did not seem to be near enough to the city to bring him into contact with others during his stay.

of your birth" (Gen 31:13). Two things come to our attention. First, God identified himself to Jacob through place association, essentially his address. This person was a specific God, the same God who appeared to Jacob at Bethel. God even reminded Jacob of his significant actions at the site.

Secondly, nothing in the text indicates ... jacob ascribed any importance to the place of this newest dream that he was recounting to his wives. This lack of significance is probably because Jacob considered Bethel to be God's primary link with the earth, thereby eliminating most other sites as appropriate for worship. This interpretation makes sense in light of Jacob's dream at Bethel. In that dream, the angels were going to and from God on the stairway. Therefore, Jacob may have viewed an angelic messenger as having come from God at Bethel (31:11). This connection was reinforced by the message of the angel who, as the mouthpiece of God,[12] stated, "I am the God of Bethel," thereby showing the importance of Bethel over other places.[13]

Later in the story (ch. 35), Jacob was told to relocate to Bethel and make an altar there.[14] On the journey there, Jacob instructed all those who were with him to purify themselves, and they buried their foreign gods.[15] No other deities would be welcomed or worshiped at Bethel. Thus, Bethel had become a permanent sacrificial site to the God of Jacob that would be administered by Jacob himself. Such action increased the status of Bethel, because its sacred nature would be visible by a physical structure and maintained by regular worship.

---

[12] There is a certain ambiguity about the speaker in Jacob's dream, who was identified as an angel and yet stated, "I am God." See the section on the burning bush above.

[13] My thanks to Dr. Richard Sarason for his helpful comments on this idea.

[14] While Jacob had anointed a "pillar" there previously, an altar was required for proper sacrifices. This was the only time when God directed a patriarch to build an altar.

[15] It is interesting to note that Jacob called for ritualistic purity from his whole entourage as he prepared to approach the sacred space of Bethel to build an altar (35:2). He firmly believed that God's potent presence was at Bethel. See Sarna, *Understanding Genesis*, 194.

In Gen 35:9–13, God revealed himself at Bethel once again and changed Jacob's name to Israel, along with reiterating the promises that he had previously made. Interestingly, it is not immediately clear that the setting was Bethel; verse 13 just uses "in the place" (בַּמָּקוֹם). However, the term "place" (מָקוֹם) could imply sacred space. Thus, the word choice makes perfect sense—it indicates the sanctity of the place in which God had just communicated with Jacob. Verse 15 ("Jacob called the place where God had talked with him Bethel") clarifies any doubt that may be left in the reader's mind as to the name of the מָקוֹם. Ultimately, the additional revelation and Jacob's act of altar building and rededication of the standing stone[16] confirmed that Bethel had a special connection with God—a connection that God initiated and Jacob memorialized.

In contrast to those temporarily sacred places we looked at in the last chapter, Bethel retained its sacred status long after Jacob's communications with God. Once the Israelites secured the land, they went to Bethel when they had a query for God. For example, when the tribes were going to war with Benjamin over the Levite's slain wife (Judges 19), they went to Bethel[17] to ask God who should take the front line against the Benjaminites. After a devastating loss in battle, the Israelites returned to Bethel and wept. Judges 20:26 states, "Then all the sons of Israel and all the people went up

---

[16] It could also be argued that the stone in question was entirely different from that of Genesis 28. However, examined from the perspective of a literary whole, rededication of the same stone makes good contextual sense. After all, such a ceremonial act would be a fitting conclusion to the cycle that had the initial anointing at its beginning (Genesis 28). This idea finds support in the Annals of Sennacherib as well. Daniel David Luckenbill, "The 'Bît Kutalli' or Armory," chap. 7 in *The Annals of Sennacherib* (Chicago: University of Chicago Press, 1924), col. 6: 76–79. "When that palace shall have become old and ruined, may some future prince restore its ruins, look upon the stela with my name inscribed (thereon), anoint it with oil, pour out a libation upon it and return it to its place." (D. D. Luckenbill, "The 'Bît Kutalli' or Armory," chap. 7 in *The Annals of Sennacherib* [Chicago: University of Chicago Press, 1924]).

[17] The reference was to the site and not to the "house of God," since "El" was never used for the God of Israel in the book of Judges. See Block, *Judges, Ruth,* 558.

and came to Bethel and wept; thus they remained there before the LORD and fasted that day until evening. And they offered burnt offerings and peace offerings before the LORD."

It is important to note that the people "remained before the LORD" (וישבו שם לפני יהוה) in a state of mourning. When the biblical author states that the people were weeping and subsequently offering sacrifices before the Lord, he is indicating that the people were in the presence of God in a way distinct from the normal routine.[18] God was accessible in a particular way at Bethel, and the people knew this. They did not stay at the battle site or even just move a safe distance away; they went where they were sure that God would hear them.[19] This is not to say that the people thought that God could not hear or see them at other places; God's awareness of the suffering of the Israelites in Egypt would contradict such an assumption. However, the connection to God at a sacred place like Bethel was certain.[20] The fact that the Israelites offered burnt offerings and peace offerings before the Lord (Judg 20:26) serves to further affirm Bethel's sacred status.

Bethel's significance as a sacred site diminished with the rise of Jerusalem, only to experience a resurgence with the division of Israel into the southern kingdom of Judah and the northern kingdom of Israel. The northern kingdom found itself in the unenviable position of having its major religious site

---

[18] Verse 27 states that the ark was present at Bethel at that time. Bethel had sacred status independent from the presence of the ark, but the presence of such a holy object no doubt increased the belief and awareness of God's accessibility at Bethel. For more on the ark's relationship to sacred space, see the preceding chapter.

[19] By the time of the temple (see 1 Kings 8 section in the previous chapter), we see the idea that prayers could be directed at a "telephone booth" from a distance. This did not seem to be the assumption prior to Solomon's dedication of the temple.

[20] This is an issue of degree. Sitting "before God" represented a more localized and more intense idea of holiness and connection, whereas God "going with someone" was an extension of God's presence and favor. It is our contention that these distinctions blur and eventually become null over time. See Gen 27:7; Exod 16:33; Deut 6:25; Josh 6:26; 1 Sam 11:15; 23:18; 26:19.

located in the capital of Judah. Jeroboam's response was to bill two sites previously known to be sacred places as centers of worship in his new kingdom. One of these centers was Bethel. Jeroboam's actions had implications for the sacred space of Bethel, which we will discuss in the next chapter.

Beersheba

Beersheba was a site near the southern border of biblical Israel, and it was another important example of a place with ongoing sanctity. Several passages illustrate its status, but two stand out. First, Genesis 26 touches on the life of Isaac and his unique relationship with Beersheba. In this passage, Isaac traveled inland to Beersheba from the coastal region surrounding Gerar. In verse 24, we see the Lord appearing to Isaac at night and restating the promise given to Abraham: "The LORD appeared to him the same night and said, 'I am the God of your father Abraham; Do not fear, for I am with you. I will bless you, and multiply your descendants, for the sake of My servant Abraham.'" The Lord identified himself via his relationship with Isaac's father, Abraham.[21] Up to this point in the narrative, neither Abraham nor Isaac seemed to have one particular place that they associated with the Lord. Therefore, the Lord identified himself through paternal association and the continuing promises and life events that were passed from father to son.[22]

Isaac's response to this revelation is immediate. He builds a מזבח or "altar."[23] Unlike Jacob's response to the revelation at Bethel, no comment is given on Isaac's emotional response. However, the building of a מזבח (altar) demonstrated Isaac's recognition that God was especially accessible at

---

[21] Waltke, *Genesis*, 370, believes that the commemorative tokens of God's blessing that Abraham set up were still at Beersheba when Isaac arrived there.

[22] There is an intentional effort to show a parallel between the lives of Abraham and Isaac in the narrative of the biblical text. If we take the comment of the narrator in Gen 26:18 at face value, then the repetition is intentional in the mind of Isaac as he moves from place to place.

[23] Verse 25. Abraham also built altars in response to divine revelation. See Gen 12:7–8.

Beersheba. While Abraham had called on the name of the Lord at Beersheba, there was never a direct revelation there (Genesis 21). Beersheba did not truly become sacred space until God's revelation to Isaac.[24]

In our second passage, we see Jacob's interesting relationship with Beersheba. In Genesis 28, he left Beersheba and traveled to Bethel. As noted above, he received a divine revelation at Bethel, and it became the main sacred place where Jacob worshiped the Lord. So, what was the relationship of Beersheba and Bethel? No doubt the author mentions the two sites for a purpose. One reason may be to show a transition from the sacred site of the father, Isaac, to a new sacred site for the son, Jacob. If we assume that this is correct, it is important to note that the change of address did not necessarily mean that the former place was no longer sacred.[25]

Jacob's later life illustrated this. In Genesis 46, Jacob returned to Beersheba and it was there, not at Bethel, that Jacob received a divine revelation:

> So Israel set out with all that he had, and came to Beersheba, and offered sacrifices to the God of his father Isaac. God spoke to Israel in visions[26] of the night and said, "Jacob, Jacob." And he said, "Here I am." He said, "I am God, the God of your father; do not be afraid to go down to Egypt, for I will make you a great nation there. I will go down with you to Egypt, and I will also surely bring you up again; and Joseph will close your eyes." (Gen 46:1–4)

---

[24] It should be noted that altars were not always built out of recognition of a place's sanctity. Nevertheless, building an altar was an appropriate response to direct revelation. Both Isaac and Jacob saw the need to designate the spaces of their revelatory experiences as distinct from their environs. Jacob set up an anointed "pillar" and Isaac built an altar.

[25] We will pick up on this idea and explore it more fully in the next chapter.

[26] Some versions have "vision" (singular). The difference rests in a small change and may represent a mistake on the part of the Masoretes. Keil, however, understands this as an intensive plural (*Pentateuch*, 237). Whether it is plural (visions) or singular (vision), it makes little difference to the idea of the narrative at this juncture.

It is significant that once Israel, or Jacob, reached Beersheba, he offered sacrifices there to "the God of his father, Isaac."[27] He did not question whether it was acceptable to offer sacrifices to God at Beersheba,[28] since he knew the site as a sacred place by virtue of the revelation that his father, Isaac (26:23–25), and grandfather, Abraham (21:32–33), received there.[29] But up to this point, Jacob had not personally received a revelation at Beersheba, like the one he received at Bethel. As a result, Jacob's sacrifice at Beersheba was offered to the God *of his father, Isaac*. It seems logical that Jacob's sacrifice at Beersheba was an acknowledgment that Bethel and Beersheba were tied to the same God.

One reason God communicated with Jacob at Beersheba is evident in the instruction that followed: God told him to go to Egypt. While God provided the necessary phone lines, he was not limited to them.[30] In the revelation at Beersheba, God demonstrated to Jacob his ability to communicate at any site he chose. Whether Jacob was in Bethel, Beersheba, or even Egypt, God could open a line of communication. Fallen humanity experienced difficulty interacting with God and required specific communication points, but God himself was not so limited.

---

[27] This Hebrew term (זבח) occurs in Genesis only here and in 31:54. Sacrifice, at its core, was an act of communication with God. Waltke, *Genesis*, 573.

[28] Jacob's story outside of the Promised Land begins and ends at Beersheba. God's revelation here resembles the revelation given to Jacob at Bethel (28:10–22). Waltke understands Jacob to be worshiping at the altar that was built by Isaac. Even if it was not the same altar, v. 1 implies Jacob was familiar with his father's cultic activity at the site. See Waltke, *Genesis*, 573.

[29] This may be behind God's initial self-identification as the "God of your father." This identification also makes God recognizable as the God of the covenant (see Walton, *Genesis*, 683).

[30] Generically speaking, the ancient Near Eastern worldview held to the existence of many gods. Each of these gods had a primary sphere of influence that was usually tied either to some aspect of nature or to geographic territory. See Daniel I. Block, *The Gods of the Nations: Studies in Ancient Near Eastern National Theology* (Winona Lake, IN: Eisenbrauns, 1988).

Gilgal

Gilgal was the Israelites' first camp after they crossed the Jordan, and it served as the major base of operations during the conquest of Canaan. After the conquest, the headquarters were transferred to Shiloh, but Gilgal remained an important site for Israel, both geographically and religiously.

The text does not seem to indicate that a revelation of place sanctity occurred directly at Gilgal. There was no dream or vision, as at Bethel and Beersheba. However, there was direct communication from God. Additionally, upon closer inspection, we see that Gilgal's special status was connected to the crossing of the Jordan River. This crossing was reminiscent of God's action at the Red Sea (Exodus 14). Indeed, Joshua 4–5 describes setting up camp at Gilgal, and the subsequent events there, as a continuation of the divine action that began with the parting of the Jordan waters:

> Now when all the nation had finished crossing the Jordan, the LORD spoke to Joshua, saying, "Take for yourselves twelve men from the people, one man from each tribe, and command them, saying, 'Take up for yourselves twelve stones from here out of the middle of the Jordan, from the place where the priests' feet are standing firm, and carry them over with you and lay them down in the lodging place where you will lodge tonight.'" (Josh 4:1–3)

Interestingly, the Lord spoke directly to Joshua and gave him instructions,[31] yet these instructions did not seem to have a visible component. The conversation did not result in the place becoming sacred. Rather, the conversational

---

[31] The direct communication that Joshua received was more intimate than those received by the patriarchs: Joshua received direct discourse, while the patriarchs received dreams. Joshua communicated with God on a regular basis, as Moses did. The difference may have been the tabernacle. Moses and Joshua may have carried on much of their conversation in the sacred space of the tabernacle, but the text does not always make this clear (see Num 7:89). As a result, it is more difficult to identify which "revelations" of God were of such caliber that they sanctified a space, as opposed to occurring in a space already known to be sacred (i.e., the tabernacle). The text often provides clues when a particular space

revelation most likely took place in the tabernacle[32] and therefore falls within the category of space that was only sacred temporarily,[33] whereas places that maintained a sacred status were often associated with a revelation that had a visible component.

Once the priests carrying the ark left the riverbed, the area became submerged under the Jordan again. Obviously, this created a problem in terms of access to the site of God's action. This is what makes God's instructions to Joshua so interesting. The twelve stones taken from the river were placed at the campsite on the western side of the Jordan. When the men placed the stones on accessible dry land, the sanctity of the place in the river was effectively transferred to Gilgal, thereby making ongoing worship at the place of revelation possible.[34]

The similarities between Bethel and Gilgal are striking. Jacob acknowledged Bethel as sacred ground by setting up a stone marker (מזבח). At Gilgal, the twelve stones were used in the same manner, but, where Jacob used one stone, Joshua used twelve to represent each of the tribes. Setting up stones to mark a sacred place was common practice in the ancient Near East. However, verse 7 states that the stones were to serve as a memorial לזכרון to succeeding generations.

---

becomes sacred, though. See for example, Josh 5:15, in which the angel of the Lord specifically stated that the ground was holy.

[32] See Exod 25:22; 26:33; 30:6, 36; Lev 16:2; Num 7:89; 10:35; Josh 7:6.

[33] See previous chapter for more on this type of sacred space.

[34] The idea of transferring sacred ground is also evident in the narrative of the Aramean general, Naaman (2 Kgs 5:17). After being cleansed of leprosy, Naaman carried back some Israelite soil to his native land, so that he might properly worship the God of Israel there. This, of course, reflected the belief that the various gods were limited to geographic regions. See Block, *Gods of the Nations*. This also has parallels with the sanctity associated with the tabernacle. The sanctity of the tabernacle was attached to the objects of the structure so that it was transferable. The stones in this narrative, however, seem only to mark the space as sacred, rather than being sacred themselves. See chapter 2 for more on the tabernacle as sacred space.

What was the difference between a sacred site and a memorial to a divine revelation or act? We can conclude from our research so far that sacred space memorialized a divine act or revelation, and in so doing, pointed to that space's special connection with God.[35] The sanctity of the site was then remembered through religious markers and regular worship, which served to reinforce the memory of the divine revelation and the knowledge that God was especially accessible there.

Joshua 5:13–15[36] tells of the encounter between Joshua and the captain of the army of the Lord "near Jericho." If this encounter was associated with the environs of Gilgal, then the revelation was perhaps a confirmation of the sanctity of the site.[37] Joshua encountered a man who was standing with

---

[35] In the case of Bethel and Beersheba, it was divine *revelation* to the patriarchs that indicated the sanctity of the site. As for Gilgal, it was the divine *action* of parting the waters of the Jordan River that initially imbued sacred status. Verses 19–23 revisit this idea and tie specifically to God's parting of the Red Sea. A question is raised: Why did Gilgal become a sacred site when there was no similar sanctification at the Red Sea? First, there was no divine command to memorialize the Red Sea crossing with stones in the Exodus narrative, as there was with the Jordan crossing. Second, Gilgal was in the land of Israel and represented a site of Israelite habitation. Third, the Exodus narrative implied that the Israelites continued their journey fairly soon after the Red Sea crossing, whereas at Gilgal, they set up a significant base of operations and underwent covenant renewal and circumcision.

[36] Some argue that the revelation continues into chapter 6. See, for example, C. J. Goslinga, *Joshua, Judges, Ruth*, Bible Student's Commentary, trans. Ray Togtman (Grand Rapids: Zondervan, 1927 (Dutch), 1986), 67. The Masoretic Text puts a break after 6:1. Even if the pericope was meant to include 6:1–5, the primary material within the revelation for establishing sacred space is 5:13–15, so we have limited our discussion to these verses.

[37] The fact that the narrative takes place "by Jericho" (M. Noth, *The Deuteronomistic History*, et al.) instead of specifically citing the name "Gilgal" is problematic and forces a reliance on the larger context in order to associate the episode with Gilgal. If we treat 5:13–15 as attached to the preceding explanation of the origin of the name for the site, the context chosen by the author could arguably point to the area being Gilgal or its environs. Much depends on the interpretation of the preposition ב. The Hebrew preposition ב has a wide range of meaning, but the context narrows this range considerably. John Gray states,

sword drawn. Apparently, there was nothing out of the ordinary about the man, except for his drawn weapon, because Joshua reacted to him as though he were a mere man. When the stranger revealed himself as the captain of the army of the Lord (שׂר־צבא־יהוה) Joshua immediately prostrated himself in a posture of worship.[38]

Verse 15 is fascinating: "The captain of the LORD's host said to Joshua, 'Remove your sandals from your feet, for the place where you are standing is holy.' And Joshua did so." The parallel to Moses's encounter with the burning bush is unmistakable. In fact, it is this very parallel that affirms the identity of this "captain" of the Lord. Exodus 3:2 states that the appearance of the angel of the Lord caused the bush to burn. However, the Lord himself spoke with Moses and declared the ground holy. Joshua's reaction to the captain showed that he believed that he was interacting with God himself and not just a messenger. The parallel command to remove his sandals because of the sanctity of the space reinforces this fact.[39] As with the burning bush, the "captain of the army of the LORD" was the outward form of a direct revelation from God.

"Such a theophany is usually associated with the authentication of a holy place (cf. Bethel, Gen 28:12), which is clearly indicated in verse 15. This might have been Gilgal, especially if 'by Jericho' (v. 13) means 'in the region of Jericho'; cf. Syriac 'in the plains of Jericho.'" John Gray, *Joshua, Judges and Ruth*, The Century Bible (London: Thomas Nelson and Sons, 1967), 71. The fact remains that the named place was Jericho rather than Gilgal. Thus, if associating the pericope with Gilgal is incorrect, and the angelic revelation did not take place in its immediate environs, then this revelatory event fits within the category of one-time sacred places (see preceding chapter).

[38] Joshua's posture and attitude of worship is important in terms of what he assumed about the identity of the "captain of the army of the LORD." In fact, Josh 5:15 duplicates the language contained in Exod 3:5. Soggin states, "Note, however, that here, as in other passages which deal with the prehistory of Israel, the angel is not a being distinct from Yahweh, but in a sense is one of his hypostases, to the extent that the worship paid to him is directed to Yahweh himself." J. Alberto Soggin, *Joshua, A Commentary*, trans. John Bowden (Philadelphia: Westminster, 1972), 78.

[39] The idea that the captain of the Lord's army was the outer form for the Lord himself was therefore present in Joshua's mind, as well as the narrator's.

If it is correct that the appearance of the captain of the army of the Lord was near Gilgal, then the event served to reinforce the other elements that testified of Gilgal's connection with God: the presence of the stones transferred from the site of God's revelation in the Jordan River (Josh 4:1–3) and the long-term resting point for the ark of the covenant (Josh 4:19).[40] Additionally, the phrase "before the LORD" is used of people at Gilgal (1 Sam 11:15; 15:33), and it is a common factor to other sacred places and revelations of God as well (Exod 6:12; 28:35; Deut 12:7–12; Josh 4:13; 18:10; 1 Sam 1:12). As with the burning bush, the area around the angel was holy ground only temporarily. The initial revelation in the river and the long-term presence of the ark at Gilgal are the key factors for the sacred status of the area.

Judges 2:1–5 records the next significant mention of Gilgal. The first phrase of the passage reveals that an angel of the Lord came up from Gilgal to a place called "Bochim."[41] This raises the question as to why a messenger came specifically from Gilgal. By the time of the judges, the ark was in Shiloh, so the divine connection to Gilgal must have come from something else.[42]

In fact, there are two likely reasons that the messenger was connected with Gilgal in this narrative. First, the nature of the message to the Israelites was integrally connected to Gilgal. The angel chastised the congregation for their failure to keep the covenant and explained that this failure was why they only partially controlled the Promised Land.[43] Gilgal was the first campsite after the Israelites crossed the Jordan and was subsequently the

---

[40] The presence of the ark and tabernacle at Gilgal are implied, since this was the Israelites' base camp for a prolonged period of time.

[41] ויעל מלאך־יהוה מן־הגלגל אל־הבכים. Bochim (literally, "weepers") is most likely a temporary and symbolic designation for the site of Bethel (See LXX) or the "Oak of Weeping" near Bethel (Gen 35:8). (See Gray, *Joshua, Judges and Ruth*, 253, and Block, *Judges, Ruth*, 112.) That the names of Gilgal and Bochim form a contrast lend support to this view (See Goslinga, *Joshua, Judges, Ruth*, 261). While Gilgal represented a favorable revelation, Bochim involved chastisement.

[42] Josh 18:1; 21:2; Judg 18:31; 21:19; 1 Sam 1:3.

[43] The divine messenger referred to several covenant stipulations in his address—specifically Exod 23:20–33 and 34:11–15.

place of covenant renewal (Joshua 4). The approach of the messenger from Gilgal served as a reminder of the covenant stipulations attached to a successful conquest.

Second, the identity of this messenger from Gilgal was important. As noted above, Joshua encountered one "captain of the army of the LORD" near Jericho.[44] The narrator may intend to link this captain with the messenger who addressed the people in Judges 2. In the same way that angels came and went on missions via the stairway connection at Bethel, so too did the captain come from Gilgal. The messenger was no doubt the same one that the Lord had promised to send ahead of the Israelites in their conquest of Canaan—that is, the captain of the army of the Lord. This captain, or angel, was really the outward form for the power and presence of God,[45] and led the Israelites in the same way he did in the wilderness (Exod 13:21). By having this messenger approach from Gilgal, the narrator effectively shows the link between what should have taken place following the initial revelation and the problematic situation currently facing the Israelites. The messenger-captain was no longer going ahead of the Israelites in their battles because of their failure to heed God's instructions.

While Gilgal remained a viable worship site into the eighth century, its status diminished over time, in part due to the removal of the ark and the shift of the political center of the country toward Shiloh in the highlands. Gilgal maintained its importance as a sacred site well into the divided kingdom period; both Elijah and Elisha used Gilgal as a base of operations (2 Kgs 2:1; 4:38). In the end, Shiloh eclipsed Gilgal and most other phone booth connections in importance, and so it is to that site that we now turn our attention.

---

[44] See above for additional discussion of the identity of this so-called captain.
[45] See Exod 23:20–23, 32:34; 33:2. In Judg 2:2–3, there is a characteristic switch to the first-person speech of God, which indicates that this was indeed a type of theophany. See J. Gordon Harris, Cheryl A. Brown, and Michael S. Moore, *NIBC: Joshua, Judges, Ruth*, Old Testament Series (Peabody, MA: Hendrickson, 2000), 152. Compare to Gray, *Joshua, Judges and Ruth*, 254.

Shiloh

More than any of the sacred places with an ongoing connection to God, Shiloh served as a predecessor to the temple of Jerusalem, since Shiloh had some form of a permanent temple structure and priests serving there.[46]

The first significant information about Shiloh comes in the book of Joshua.[47] Chapter 18 records the transfer of the tabernacle and government from Gilgal, the war camp, to Shiloh. Interestingly, the narrative gives no reason why Shiloh was chosen. Whereas regarding most holy sites, the text depicts some kind of self-revelation by God, in Shiloh none was present.

In Joshua 18, we see that Joshua instructed those who were mapping the land to return to him at Shiloh, so he could cast lots before the Lord.[48] The significant phrase occurs in verse 8: ופה אשליך לכם גורל לפני יהוה בשלה ("then I will cast lots for you here before the LORD in Shiloh").[49] Given the context of the chapter, the most obvious interpretation is that this phrase referred to the tabernacle at Shiloh. Yet, it is strange that the tabernacle was not mentioned, while Shiloh was.[50] It was only after the lots had been cast and the territories determined that the tabernacle's role was mentioned

---

[46] See Marten H. Woudstra, *The Ark of the Covenant from Conquest to Kingship* (Philadelphia: Presbyterian and Reformed, 1965), for an alternate view. Woudstra argues that the language of 1 Samuel must be read as referring to the tent structure of the tabernacle alone.

[47] "Shiloh" (שילה) may be mentioned in Gen 49:10, although this is debated. For a discussion and bibliography of the many views that have been put forth on this *crux interpretum*, see Wenham, *Genesis 16–50*, 476–78, and *New Bible Dictionary* (Wheaton: Tyndale House, 1991), s.v. "Shiloh."

[48] Donald G. Schley, *Shiloh: A Biblical City in Tradition and History* (Sheffield, England: Sheffield Academic Press, 1989), 130. Schley argues that this phrase (before the Lord/God) is usually indicative of the presence of a temple or cult site.

[49] Similar phrasing occurs in v. 6, but lacks the specific reference to Shiloh.

[50] Shiloh is mentioned three times in these verses, whereas the tent of meeting is not mentioned once. The emphasis on the place of Shiloh is clear. Compare with Trent C. Butler, *Joshua*, Word Biblical Commentary, ed. David A. Hubbard, Glenn W. Barker, John D. Watts (Dallas: Word Books, 1984), 204–5. Butler understands the emphasis to be on the tent of meeting here. Shiloh is emphasized in 1 Sam 3:21 as well (see below).

(Josh 19:51). Joshua 18:8–10 simply delineates that the Lord was present at Shiloh, and that he controlled the outcome of the lots. Even though the passage does not mention divine self-revelation, Shiloh would become to the landed tribes of Israel what Gilgal was to the conquering tribes of Israel. Issues concerning the whole nation were to be addressed "before the LORD" at Shiloh.[51]

The bulk of scriptural texts that testify to Shiloh's sanctity come from 1 Samuel 1–4. Several verses testify to the established religious institutions at Shiloh. In 1:3 the narrative states, "Now this man [Elkanah] would go up from his city yearly to worship and to sacrifice to the LORD of hosts in Shiloh. And the two sons of Eli, Hophni and Phinehas, were priests to the LORD there." The first item to be noted is the fact that the man went to Shiloh to sacrifice and worship each year. This clearly illustrated God's connection with Shiloh. The second item of import is that Shiloh had functioning priests. Shiloh was an active worship center and not just a simple altar. This, of course, would have been a natural product of the presence of the tabernacle and ark at Shiloh.[52]

In 1 Sam 1:9, we read that Eli the priest was resting near the "doorpost of the temple of the LORD" על־מזוזה היכל יהוה. This little phrase indicates that some form of permanent structure had been built, either to supplement the tabernacle or to replace it (the shift from a tabernacle to a formal temple [היכל] may indicate that more permanent buildings were erected to complement the tent of the tabernacle).[53] Whatever the case, the people clearly assumed that the sacred status of Shiloh was ongoing and that God was

---

[51] However, this is not exclusive to Shiloh, as is evident in Josh 24:1, in which the tribes were "before God" at Shechem.

[52] The ark and tabernacle were moved from Gilgal to Shiloh at some point during the period of the judges. See Judg 18:31.

[53] Later in the same chapter (v. 24), the text refers to the "house of the LORD" (בית־יהוה). However, the biblical text sometimes refers to the tabernacle this way. See, for example, Josh 6:24. Also note 2 Sam 7:6, which indicates that the structure here was not on the level of a formal temple.

especially present there, since some manner of "home" had been built for him that incorporated more substantial structures than just the tent of meeting.[54]

Two other passages demonstrate that Shiloh had a fully developed worship site. 1 Samuel 2:12–14 describes the practice of the priests with regard to sacrifices. While the description is in the context of condemnation of the sinful acts of corrupt priests, the passage still testifies to an established religious system. In fact, the narration assumes that the corrupt acts were within the sight and presence of the Lord and were offensive to him (1 Sam 2:17).

One of the most significant passages pertaining to the sacred status of Shiloh is 1 Samuel 3, which relates the story of God's calling to Samuel at Shiloh. Interestingly, the chapter initiates the narrative episode with the caveat that divine revelation had become rare. The narrative does not elaborate on whether this rarity was something that plagued the nation as a whole or was isolated to Shiloh. Taking context into consideration, namely the evil behavior of Eli's sons at the sanctuary, Shiloh was likely the "epicenter" of the dearth of revelation.[55] Ultimately, this lack of revelation was the literary backdrop for the changing situation.

In verses 2–14, God revealed himself to Samuel, thereby breaking the divine silence, and told Samuel of the downfall of the house of Eli. What draws our attention is the comment that followed this revelation[56] in verse 21: "And the LORD continued to appear at Shiloh: the LORD revealed

---

[54] The idea behind a temple in the ancient Near East was that of a dwelling place for the deity on earth. First Kings 8 underscores the paradox of this idea for a deity who is omnipresent.

[55] The fact that the narrator points out the lack of divine revelation may be an indicator that it was an abnormal condition for Shiloh. The ambiguity stems from the difficulty of how to translate the final word in v. 1: נפרץ. This word is usually associated with a calamity of some sort or with a breach in a wall. Either aspect of meaning might work in our context, but the overall negative implication is clear. See Godfrey Rolles Driver, "The Root פרץ. in Hebrew," *Journal of Theological Studies* 25, no. 98 (January 1924): 177–78.

[56] Since the Lord "stood by Samuel" (ויבא יהוה ויתיצב), this should be understood as a vision and not just an auditory revelation. Cf. Gen 28:13; Exod 34:5; Job 4:16.

Himself to Samuel at Shiloh with the word of the LORD."[57] Prior to this passage, there was no recorded, direct self-revelation from God in association
with Shiloh; the tabernacle seemed to be the primary sanctifying element.

Verse 21 removes any doubt about Shiloh's status as a sacred place.
Shiloh appears first in the verse, even before Samuel's name. The narrator
emphasizes *where* God revealed himself to Samuel.[58] God's ongoing revelation now characterized the place.[59] Samuel then took the messages that he
received out to Israel, and the people came to consult him. This message
dispersal paralleled Jacob's vision at Bethel; in that vision, the angels had
their dispersal point at Bethel. Bethel was the contact point for God, and
the message went out from there. Shiloh seemed to have a similar quality,
but instead of angels, Samuel was the messenger. Shiloh had become the
major point of contact between God and Israel.

First Samuel 4 seems to be distinct from chapters 1–3 in many ways,
but there are themes that connect the two sections. Chapter 4 tells of the
removal of the ark from Shiloh and its loss to the Philistines. Within the
chapter, verse 4 is important for our discussion: "So the people sent to
Shiloh, and from there they carried the ark of the covenant of the LORD
of hosts who sits above the cherubim; and the two sons of Eli, Hophni
and Phinehas, were there with the ark of the covenant of God." Here we
have a clear statement of the idea that the Lord dwelled in a localized sense
above the cherubim on the ark of the covenant. As long as the ark was at
Shiloh, other revelations aside, the Lord was understood to be there as well.

---

[57] Jewish Publication Society Tanakh 1985. This translation is preferable to
the New American Standard on this verse.

[58] This emphasis supports the idea that the lack of revelation noted by the
narrator in 3:1 was indeed particular to Shiloh. A lack of revelation at a place
where God was understood to dwell (tabernacle) would be noteworthy, and
would fit well with the wickedness perpetrated by Eli's sons. In this context, v. 21
overturns the problematic lack of revelation that introduced the pericope.

[59] André Caquot and Philippe de Robert, *Commentaire de L'Ancien Testament:
Les Livres de Samuel* (Genève: Labor et Fides, 1994), 70. The Hebrew emphasizes
the repetitive nature of this revelation to Samuel at Shiloh through the use of the
root יסף.

Naturally, the loss of the ark to the Philistines, which occurred later in the chapter, presented a theological crisis for the people of Israel. The very idea that motivated the people to bring the ark from Shiloh to the battle implied that God had, in some sense, left Shiloh with the sacred object. The people would be unsure if the phone line at Shiloh was still active, since there was uncertainty about the place's sanctity without the presence of the ark. The ark did not seem to return to Shiloh after its capture and subsequent return by the Philistines, leaving its status as a sacred space somewhat ambiguous.[60]

The last positive reference to Shiloh comes from 1 Kgs 14:2. In this verse, Jeroboam sent his wife to consult the prophet Ahijah, who was based at Shiloh. While we cannot derive too much from the 1 Kings reference, it is significant for our discussion that a prophet who received revelation from God was based at Shiloh. This, of course, is reminiscent of Samuel. Therefore, at least in a limited sense, Shiloh retained some level of religious significance, and perhaps even sanctity, into the early divided kingdom.[61] This was not to last, but that is a subject for the next chapter.

Conclusions

Our examination of the above sacred places illustrates several conclusions about biblical ideas of sacred space. First, and perhaps most significant, is that a particular space became sacred primarily through the self-revelation of God in that space. The vision/dream of Jacob of the stair between heaven and earth at Bethel is a good example.

---

[60] The site itself may have experienced some form of destruction as the Philistines pressed their victory, but the biblical text does not record this, and the archaeological data is ambiguous. If Shiloh was destroyed shortly after the loss of the ark, this would have been considered a sign of divine abandonment.

[61] See Otto Eissfeldt, "Silo und Jerusalem," *VTSupp* 4 (1957): 138–47, and Martin Noth, "Samuel und Silo," *VT* 13, no. 4 (October 1963): 399, for further evidence that Shiloh's sacred status continued on some level, even with the rise of Jerusalem.

Second, sacred objects could give a place a sacred association, if they remained for an extended period of time. For example, the extended presence of the ark at Shiloh encouraged the idea that it was sacred.

Third, within the land held by the twelve tribes of Israel, worship memorialized the association of God with particular places. Deuteronomy 12 indicates that a place where God revealed himself was a place where he was accessible and would accept worship. Those matters needing the confirmation of God, such as the investiture of a king, would naturally be held at a known sacred place. Worship could recognize or confirm God's particular presence in a place, but it could not confer sanctity in and of itself.

Finally, Gilgal and Beersheba illustrate that known sacred sites did not depend on Israelite possession in order to retain their sacred status. This is in keeping with the idea that sacred space was determined by God and not man. The revelation at Beersheba underscores that God is not limited to a particular place, though he may be especially present there. His power and presence went with the ones to whom he revealed himself. This is a concept that will have growing importance in our discussion of God's rejection of sacred space.

CHAPTER 5

"GO NOW TO SHILOH"

Divine Rejection of Sacred Space

Introduction

We have shown that the unifying factor among different types of sacred space is their sanctity derived from God's self-revelation. Certain sites, such as Bethel and Shiloh, had a connection with God that went beyond his initial revelation. The worshiper could return repeatedly with the assurance that God would be present and accessible at these sites. However, we have seen hints in earlier chapters that these sites did not maintain their link to heaven indefinitely; the link could be broken. Just as a place could become sacred for an extended period of time, it could also lose this sacred status if God chose to abandon it, removing the phone booth.

This chapter will explore the reasons for the loss of connection between God and his divinely sanctioned phone booths. We will address some key questions: What factors led to God rejecting a sacred space? Were the sites left standing, even though connection with God had been cut off, or were they destroyed? And finally, what were the consequences of this divine rejection, as more and more phone booths were removed?

Divine Rejection: Gilgal and Beersheba

Both Gilgal and Beersheba were rejected by God, but the biblical text does not explicitly record their physical destruction. Beersheba's initial sanctification came through God's revelation to Isaac there (Gen 26:23–25). By the kingship of Josiah in 2 Kgs 23:8, however, Beersheba was listed among the desecrated high places. Gilgal initially achieved sacred status through a combination of revelatory events and the presence of the tabernacle and ark of the covenant. The earliest negative reference to worship at Gilgal is 1 Sam 15:21–22, in which Saul's offer to sacrifice the spoils of war to God at Gilgal was rejected because of his disobedience.[1] It is important to emphasize that this rejection was aimed specifically at Saul and his proposed sacrifice, not at Gilgal as a legitimate point of contact with God; however, the rejected sacrifice ultimately foreshadowed the rejection of Gilgal itself. Saul's disobedience led to God's rejection of him as king; we will see that disobedience is closely tied to God's rejection of a site.

God's rejection of Gilgal occurred during the prophetic careers of Hosea and Amos, with the rejection of Beersheba isolated to the book of Amos. Hosea and Amos were the earliest literary prophets and were contemporaries, although their books show no direct awareness of one another. Amos most likely issued his oracles late in the reign of Jeroboam II, based on the level of affluence that he ascribed to the northern kingdom. There is one brief autobiographical narrative delineating his conflict with Amaziah at Bethel (7:10–17).

Hosea prophesied from approximately 750 BC until the fall of the northern kingdom in 722–721. He started his prophetic ministry during the reign of Jeroboam II and was primarily concerned with the northern kingdom of Israel. There are three citations in Hosea that, taken collectively, describe the rejection of Gilgal. The first verse, Hos 4:15, is an injunction against going to Gilgal to worship God: "Though you, Israel, play the

---

[1] The rejection technically came from Samuel, but in light of the larger context, Samuel was merely God's representative. See especially 1 Sam 15:1, 10–11.

harlot, do not let Judah become guilty; also do not go to Gilgal, or go up to Beth-aven and take the oath: 'As the LORD lives!'"[2] The verse offers no clarification on what the offensive worship was, but the oath "as the LORD lives," may offer a clue. While such an oath seems to have been a common way to declare oneself accountable, a few commentators speculate that the oath was being used in the Baal fertility rituals at Gilgal.[3] Whether or not this is the case, the larger context makes it clear that the people were engaging in non-Yahwistic, immoral cultic activity.

Hosea 9:15 describes this illicit worship at Gilgal more fully: "All their evil is at Gilgal; indeed, I came to hate them there! Because of the wickedness of their deeds, I will drive them out of My house! I will love them no more; all their princes are rebels." The important question is "Why Gilgal?" Why didn't Hosea pick any other shrine where false worship was being practiced? The most logical explanation is Gilgal's link to many of God's historical acts. It was Israel's initial camp after the crossing of the Jordan and a place where God revealed himself (Josh 4:19). It was at Gilgal that Israel was dedicated before the Lord through the rite of circumcision (Josh 5:8–9). It was also the place where Saul was confirmed by the Israelites before the Lord and, ultimately, rejected by him (1 Sam 11:15; 13:12–15). Collectively, these events show that Gilgal was a sacred place—an access point to communicate with God. This made the "evil" at the site more significant than if it were at a site with no special connection to the God of Israel. Worship of foreign gods

---

[2] The textual apparatus of the BHS suggests that the whole verse is a later addition, borrowed from Amos 5:5 and 8:14. However, the similarity in language between the two can be attributed to subject matter and similar context. See Douglas Stuart, *Word Biblical Commentary 31: Hosea–Jonah* (Dallas: Word, 1987), 84. Beth-aven is a derogatory term for Bethel here. We will revisit this in the discussion on Bethel.

[3] See Elizabeth Achtemeier, *NIBC: Minor Prophets 1*, ed. Robert L. Hubbard and Robert K. Johnson (Peabody, MA: Hendrickson, 1999); James Luther Mays, *Hosea: A Commentary*, Old Testament Library (Philadelphia: Westminster, 1969); Thomas Edward McComiskey, ed., *Hosea*, in *The Minor Prophets: An Exegetical and Expository Commentary*, vol. 1 (Grand Rapids: Baker, 1992). McComiskey disagrees.

at Gilgal amounted to a traitorous denial of God's acts on Israel's behalf. The rejection of Saul as king was a result of his effort to manipulate God at a divinely sanctioned communication point. The leaders condemned by Hosea likely held the same misconception as Saul: they believed they could manipulate God through illegitimate sacrifice.

The main issue in Hosea was the false worship of other gods. This is not to say that the kingship did not factor into the divine rejection of Gilgal, only that it was not the primary factor. Nowhere else did Hosea regard the institutional monarchy as the reason for God's judgment on the nation. Thus, the evil cited in the verse must refer to something else. The evil should be understood with its consequence: the idea that God "came to hate them there." The "evil" referred to in the verse has some history at Gilgal. The biblical story (Judg 2:6–3:6) tells that the generation following Joshua's engaged in the worship of the Baals.[4] Indeed, the context of Hosea 9 refers to the moral corruption and civil war that plagued Israel in Judges 19–21.[5] It was likely this same sort of moral and religious corruption was characterized by the word *evil* at Gilgal.[6] This is confirmed in the second half of the verse, which cites "the wickedness of their deeds" as a parallel to "their evil."

The result of the corruption at Gilgal was removal of the people from God's "house." This house was most likely a physical structure. Given the long history of worship at Gilgal, it would not be unusual for a building to have been erected. Hosea gave no clarification on this point; the house might have just been a metaphor here for the land of Israel.[7] Whatever the case, it is safe to assume that "house" does not refer to the Jerusalem temple, which would be contextually discordant.

---

[4] See Achtemeier, *NIBC: Minor Prophets 1*, 83.

[5] Hosea 9:9 mentions Gibeah, which is a reference to the narrative of Judges 19–21.

[6] I am indebted to Dr. David Weisberg for a personal conversation wherein he brought to my attention that the root פעל, usually translated "to do/make" or "deed" in the nominal form, is often associated with moral consequence in Hosea.

[7] See 8:1 for a metaphorical usage of the term "house."

Hosea 12:11 (Heb 12:12) reads, "Since Gilead is wickedness, surely they shall come to nothing. In Gilgal they sacrifice bulls, so their altars will be like the stone heaps beside the furrows of the field."[8] Here we learn that bull sacrifice occurred at Gilgal.[9] This practice was not necessarily unacceptable, but here it was set in a negative context. Thus, the sacrifices in question must have been offered to the Baals. The verb זבח reinforces this conclusion, because Hosea usually used this root in association with pagan sacrifice.[10] The perfect aspect of the Piel indicates this kind of worship was habitual and characteristic of the people at Gilgal, which is why the God of Israel "came to hate them there" (9:15).

The prediction that the altars of Gilgal would become stone heaps beside a plowed field is interesting.[11] The metaphor is that of a farmer who, while plowing his field, stopped occasionally to remove a stone and throw it onto a nondescript pile on the side of the field. The stones had no particular purpose and were seen as refuse. Such would be the ultimate end of the altars at Gilgal.[12]

There is more to this analogy, however, than a simple prediction of the destruction of a place of worship. The language describing the heaps of

---

[8] My translation. I am indebted to the insights of T. McComiskey for much of the translation of this verse. See McComiskey, *Hosea,* 208. Karl Elliger in the *BHS* lists the initial אם as a corruption, suggesting עם or ב instead.

[9] Another possible interpretation is they were sacrificing to images of the bull, which would be sufficient cause for the condemnation. I am grateful to Dr. Richard Sarason for this suggestion. Elliger (*BHS*) suggests emending שורים (cattle/bulls) to לשדים (demons).

[10] Cf. 4:13–14; 11:2; 13:2. See McComiskey, *Hosea,* 209.

[11] The phrase concerning Gilead is a verbless clause followed by information concerning Gilgal, which does have a verb. Due to this syntactical break between Gilead and Gilgal, I understand the last half of the verse to be connected solely to Gilgal. For more information on the syntactical features in this verse, see McComiskey, *Hosea,* 209.

[12] The phrase referring to the altars of Gilgal is a verbless clause and is contextually ambiguous concerning its time frame. As a result, it has been translated variously as past, present, and future. I have translated it in the future time, as a prophetic prediction.

stones is reminiscent of the initial association of God with Gilgal. The word
כגלים (stone heaps) is an alliterative play on the place name of Gilgal (גלגל),
which initially referred to the rite of circumcision that took place there (Josh
5:9). However, in the narrative of Joshua 4, the camp of Gilgal was established after the miraculous crossing of the Jordan River. To commemorate
God's intervention, the Israelites were instructed to take twelve stones from
the bottom of the riverbed and place them at Gilgal. These stones were
reminders of God's action and presence there. Thus, in the book of Joshua,
we have an initial pile of stones serving to mark Gilgal as sacred space; in
Hosea, we find piles of stones representing all that was left of the altars of
Gilgal. The initial stones symbolized God's salvific act at that place; the latter stones symbolized his rejection of it.

While there was a collective aspect to the condemnation aimed at both
Gilgal and Gilead, Gilgal was selected for divine rejection because of its special status. Its condemnation and rejection cannot be viewed as just a "type"
for the nation's sin.[13] The rejection of Gilgal was the undoing of its special
connection with God and represented, at the very least, a loss of Israel's
guaranteed access to God. There was one less phone booth in the land.

In addition to the loss of connection, Hosea predicted the removal of
the people from Gilgal (9:15); they would be cast back into the wilderness.
The latter idea was a particularly ominous reversal. Not only would the
people be cut off from communication with God at that particular site,
but they would also be returned to a homeless state similar to the wilderness wanderings. There would be no tabernacle this time.[14] Thus, Hosea's
depiction of God's rejection of Gilgal related a revoking of the special connection between Israel and her God. The loss of sacred space meant the loss
of connection.

---

[13] Contrary to McComiskey, *Hosea,* 154.

[14] To use a modern analogy, we can relate this to someone living in a city with
a single phone booth. The person is then removed to an untamed region with no
means for calling for help and no real hope of rescue.

The book of Amos includes Beersheba with Gilgal in its list of sacred places condemned by God.[15] As with Hosea, there are three significant verses: 4:4; 5:5; and 8:14. Amos 4:4 states, "Enter Bethel and transgress; in Gilgal multiply transgression! Bring your sacrifices every morning, your tithes every three days." The idea here is clear: worship at Bethel or Gilgal was sinful. The protest of Amos, according to Elizabeth Achtemeier, was against those who offered their sacrifices as a means of showing off their wealth.[16] Jeffrey Niehaus, on the other hand, identifies the words of Amos as ironic exaggeration. He states, "In their zeal to offer sacrifices more frequently than required by the law, they actually increased their rebellion."[17] The more frequent offerings only accomplished greater sin; the worship at Gilgal was counted as iniquity and hindered communication with God.

Amos 5:5 contains a condemnation of Bethel, Gilgal, and Beersheba: "But do not seek Bethel, and to Gilgal do not go, and to Beersheba do not cross over, for Gilgal will surely go into exile, and Bethel will become nothing."[18] It is important to note that this verse is set in the context of a command to seek the Lord and live.[19] Yet verse 5 states that seeking the Lord at Gilgal and Beersheba was no longer acceptable. The prohibition against going to any of these shrines is emphatic in the text.[20] The command against going to these places seems to have been addressed primarily to a northern audience. For an Israelite to make a pilgrimage to Beersheba, he would truly have to "cross over" (עבר) the border into Judah. Beersheba was linked

---

[15] Amos also discussed Bethel, but we will revisit this when we examine Bethel and Shiloh below.

[16] Achtemeier, *Minor Prophets 1*, 199.

[17] Jeffrey Niehaus, *Amos*, in *The Minor Prophets: An Exegetical and Expository Commentary*, ed. Thomas Edward McComiskey (Grand Rapids: Baker, 1992), 1: 396.

[18] My translation.

[19] Verses 4 and 6.

[20] לא versus אל plus the jussive, which is a stronger command, indicating a permanent prohibition. See *GKC* §107o. Both Gilgal and Beersheba are accusatives of place, indicating that direction toward them was forbidden. See *GKC* §118d–f.

to the patriarchs—Abraham worshiped God there, and Beersheba was a point of contact between God and Isaac and Jacob. Amos 5:5, however, sets going to Beersheba, Gilgal, and Bethel as the antithesis of seeking God. The people were no longer to seek God or even his word at these places, for God was no longer accessible there.

In 5:5, Niehaus understands Amos to be drawing a distinction between the concept of the surrounding peoples that the deity may be localized and the notion that God is Spirit, not limited to any one place.[21] Thus, to "seek me and live" was to seek the Spirit of God, rather than a particular place. While these verses in Amos may contain the initial seeds of such a contrast, the contrast is overdrawn. The contention of Amos is that seeking God was, as it always has been, of crucial importance for the life of the nation. However, the places where God was once accessible were no longer available, because they had been compromised. As with the loss of the garden of Eden, communicating with God became more difficult because of sin. The next verse referring to Beersheba bears this out.

Amos 8:14 states, "As for those who swear by the guilt of Samaria, who say, 'As your god lives, O Dan,' and, 'As the way of Beersheba lives,' they will fall and not rise again." There are three elements in this verse, followed by a pronouncement that applies to all three. The first element, "the guilt of Samaria," is most likely a reference to the general worship of Baal. The second element, "as your god lives, O Dan," refers to the golden calf set up at Dan by Jeroboam.

The third and final element, "as the way of Beersheba lives," interests us the most: it seems strange to swear by such an intangible concept as "the way" (דרך). There are three options for interpreting this word. Stuart has suggested that the Ugaritic term *drkt* should be used to aid the translation of דרך in this verse.[22] The term *drkt* means dominion or might; Stuart thus

[21] Niehaus, *Amos*, 396.

[22] Stuart, *Hosea–Jonah*, 382. See also Cyrus H. Gordon, *Ugaritic Textbook*, Analetica Orientalia 38 (Rome: Pontifical Biblical Institute, 1965) and Mitchell J. Dahood, "Hebrew-Ugaritic Lexicography II," *Biblica* 45, no. 3 (1964): 404.

translates the phrase "as the power of Beersheba." This would be a unique rendering for the Hebrew, however, and remains unlikely.

Another option is to emend the text and subsequently translate the term on the basis of the Ugaritic *dr*. This would render the word "your circle/assembly (of gods)" and would indicate a pantheon of some sort.[23] The difficulty in this interpretation is that while there was certainly rampant syncretism in Israel—and more specifically Beersheba—it was never spoken of in terms of a full-blown pantheon being honored at a particular site. Thus, this translation remains problematic.

The final possibility, and perhaps the most logical conclusion, is to take the phrasing at face value and assume that the awkwardness is centered in the Western reader's perception. Taking an oath by the life of an inanimate concept may have been standard *modus operandi* for Amos's audience. Niehaus cites the current Arab practice of swearing by inanimate objects in support of this. For example, an Arab might swear by "the life of this fire" or "by this coffee!" Furthermore, Moslems swear by "the sacred way to Mecca," which is a strong parallel to Amos 8:14.[24] Assuming the translation "way" is correct, it is best to understand this as a reference to a regular pilgrimage Israelites made to Beersheba. Given the context, the pilgrimage was likely pagan. Israel had come to trust in their own cultic practices at the sites, rather than in the God of Israel.[25] In other words, religion had become more important than God.

Both Gilgal and Beersheba were acknowledged as legitimate points of contact between God and the community of Israel at some point in the nation's history.[26] This connection was established through the self-revelation of God. By the time of Amos and Hosea, however, God had rejected these sites.

---

[23] The Ugaritic term is found most frequently in the context of narrative about a pantheon of gods. See Frank J. Neuberg, "An Unrecognized Meaning of Hebrew *dor*," *JNES* 9, no. 4 (1950): 215–17, and Peter R. Ackroyd, "The Meaning of the Hebrew דוֹר Considered," *JSS* 13, no. (Spring 1968): 3–10.

[24] Niehaus, *Amos*, 477.

[25] See Achtemeier, *NIBC: Minor Prophets I*, 228.

[26] See chapter 3.

The problem with both sites that led to God's rejection centers on the worship of the people. The text characterizes this worship in terms of disobedience, which harks back, at least in terms of Gilgal, to Saul's effort to manipulate God. Furthermore, the worship at Gilgal and Beersheba was characterized by blending the worship of the Lord with the worship of the Baals from early in their history. These two issues came together to produce syncretistic, illegitimate worship that was assumed to curry the favor of the god(s) worshiped. Thus, the connection that God established at Gilgal and Beersheba was categorically reversed. The sites were divinely rejected, just as they had been divinely selected.

A Slow Fade: Bethel

We turn now to the material surrounding the rejection of Bethel and Shiloh. These two sites were both physically destroyed as part of God's rejection. The biblical text gives us more information concerning Bethel's rejection and destruction than that of the others.

The first negative references to Bethel come from 1 Kings 12–13. Jeroboam was installed as king of the newly independent northern kingdom. Out of concern that his people might regret their decision to dissolve the union if they went to Jerusalem to worship, he set up worship sites within his borders at Bethel and Dan. "So the king consulted, and made two golden calves, and he said to them, 'It is too much for you to go up to Jerusalem; behold your gods, O Israel, that brought you up from the land of Egypt.' He set one in Bethel, and the other he put in Dan" (1 Kgs 12:28–29). There is much discussion on the nature of the golden calves. Some scholars suggest that they were meant to function as footstools or thrones for various deities, and perhaps even for Yahweh, the God of Israel.[27]

---

[27] This argument is based on reliefs from the ancient Near East wherein a god is depicted as standing on the back of a bull wielding thunderbolts. See Jesse C. Long, *1 & 2 Kings*, College Press NIV Commentary: Old Testament Series, ed. Terry Briley and Paul Kissling (Joplin, MO: College Press, 2002), 165.

Others understand the calves to be syncretistic localizations of Yahweh, or even objects lacking any association with him.[28] The Hebrew text uses the plural form אלהיך (your gods), thereby interpreting Jeroboam's actions as the equivalent of installing idols. Thus, Jeroboam ironically associated his worship sites with Aaron and the golden calf.

The remaining few verses of chapter 12 make it clear that the calves were a form of illegitimate worship:

> Now this thing became a sin, for the people went to worship before the one as far as Dan. And he made houses[29] on high places, and made priests from among all the people who were not of the sons of Levi. Jeroboam instituted a feast in the eighth month on the fifteenth day of the month, like the feast which is in Judah, and he went up to the altar; thus he did in Bethel, sacrificing to the calves which he had made. And he stationed in Bethel the priests of the high places which he had made. Then he went up to the altar which he had made in Bethel on the fifteenth day in the eighth month, even in the month which he had devised in his own heart; and he instituted a feast for the sons of Israel and went up to the altar to burn incense. (1 Kgs 12:30–33)

Clearly, the installation and worship of the calves was sinful.[30] Interestingly, the text only mentions Dan. We can see good reason for the omission of

---

[28] See Klaus Koenen, *Bethel: Geschichte, Kult und Theologie*, Orbis Biblicus et Orientalis 192 (Freiburg: Universitätsverlag; Göttingen: Vandenhoeck & Ruprecht, 2003).

[29] The noun *house* or temple (בית) is singular here, but should be taken as plural in construct with the plural במות. So Noth, but see DeVries, *1 Kings*, 161.

[30] The JPS and NASB both interpret the clause as a clarification of the introductory nominal clause by translating the *waw* of the narrative preterite as "for." I agree with this interpretation, but the Hebrew syntax remains difficult. The NIV drops any translation for the *waw* and provides a semicolon between the two phrases. The LXX translates the *waw* literally with the Greek *kai* but adds the phrase "and left the house of the Lord," indicating that it too sees the second clause as explanatory.

Bethel, if we consider the difference between the two: Dan was not considered sacred, since God had not revealed himself there. Thus, the worship of the God of Israel, let alone any other deity, would have been taboo at Dan. Bethel, on the other hand, was a sacred site by virtue of God's revelation there. This distinction was possibly in the author's mind when he singled out the calf at Dan. There can be no certainty on this point, but it remains intriguing.

Verses 31–33 solidify the idea that Jeroboam was instituting a new state-sponsored religion. In fact, the first clause of verse 31 supports the idea that Bethel's absence in the previous verse was deliberate. The implication is, like Dan, the "high places" of Jeroboam had no previous association with the God of Israel. Jeroboam was probably attempting to set up a religion with strong ties to the traditions of Israel. The priesthood at Dan stemmed from a grandson of Moses (Judg 18:30–31),[31] and Bethel had ties to the Aaronides (Judg 20:26–28) and the patriarchs.[32] Likewise, both the choice of image and Jeroboam's very words reflect those of Aaron in Exod 32:4.[33] Whatever his intentions, the remainder of chapter 12 explains that every aspect of Jeroboam's cult was illegitimate.[34] The phrase, "Thus he did in Bethel, sacrificing to the calves which he had made" (1 Kgs 12:32) is particularly telling, because it shows that, in the narrator's view, Jeroboam's

---

[31] The assessment of this episode within the text is negative as well, but the genealogical link with Moses was important enough to be mentioned by the narrator.

[32] See Long, *1 & 2 Kings*, 165.

[33] "He took this from their hand, and fashioned it with a graving tool and made it into a molten calf; and they said, 'This is your god, O Israel, who brought you up from the land of Egypt.'"

[34] DeVries, *1 Kings*, 163, argues that Jeroboam was simply following an alternate calendar, having just come from Egypt, that was out of sync with the Jerusalemite calendar (which required an intercalary month every three years). Thus, Jeroboam was not creating a new religious calendar, so much as expressing independence from Jerusalem. He would have still celebrated the Feast of Tabernacles in the seventh month, as required by Num 29:12–39, but this would have been the eighth month by Jerusalemite reckoning.

sacrifices were made to man-made idols, not the God of Israel. However, Jeroboam's actions were similar to Solomon's when he built the temple. Both Solomon and Jeroboam approached the altar, something normally reserved for the priests.[35] The difference, of course, was that Jeroboam lacked the divine commission to do so.[36]

Jeroboam's actions at Bethel call into question the site's status as sacred space. Bethel had a divine connection stemming from the revelation to Jacob. However, Jeroboam's installation of the golden calf effectively introduced a foreign "name" to the place.[37] So, did Bethel continue to function as a sacred place for those who worshiped Yahweh alone? In chapter 13, a "man of God" came from Judah to Bethel and decried the altar upon which Jeroboam was offering sacrifices. Verses 1–6 relate the episode:

> Now behold, there came a man of God from Judah to Bethel by the word of the LORD, while Jeroboam was standing by the altar to burn incense. He cried against the altar by the word of the LORD, and said, "O altar, altar, thus says the LORD, 'Behold, a son shall be born to the house of David, Josiah by name; and on you he shall sacrifice the priests of the high places who burn incense on you, and human bones shall be burned on you.'" Then he gave a sign the same day, saying, "This is the sign which the LORD has spoken, 'Behold, the altar shall be split apart and the ashes which are on it shall be poured out.'" Now when the king heard the saying of the man of God, which he cried against the altar in Bethel, Jeroboam stretched out his hand from the altar, saying, "Seize him." But his hand which he stretched out against him dried up, so that he could not draw it back to himself. The altar also was split apart and the ashes were poured out from the altar, according to the sign which the man of God had given by the word of the LORD. The king said

---

[35] See section on 1 Kings 8 in chapter 2 for an explanation regarding Solomon's approach.

[36] Long, *1 & 2 Kings*, 165.

[37] See Deut 12:2-32.

to the man of God, "Please entreat the LORD your God, and pray
for me, that my hand may be restored to me." So the man of God
entreated the LORD, and the king's hand was restored to him, and
it became as it was before.

First of all, the man of God came from Judah rather than Jerusalem.[38] This
bit of information reveals that the concern of the text is with the nature of
worship at Bethel, rather than with Bethel as a competitor to Jerusalem.
The man of God cried against the altar "by the word of the LORD." This was
bona fide divine condemnation. The altar was an implement for the worship of the god represented at the site, and its condemnation was a rejection
of the worship associated with it.

The man of God proceeded to predict the destruction of the altar, both
at the moment of the prophetic condemnation, and in the future, at the
hands of Josiah. The important feature is the symbolism of this destruction. The loss of an altar effectively severed communication with the god
in question. However, the man of God's prediction went beyond the mere
destruction to actual desecration of the altar. While the immediate sign, the
altar "being split asunder" (נקרע), made it unusable for a time, the future
destruction would include the burning of human bones on the altar, a desecrating act.[39] The bones were those of the priests from Jeroboam's high
places. Thus, this prediction was a clear divine rejection of Bethel's place and
personnel. Indeed, that a descendant of David would be the one to bring
about this desecration might have indicated a rejection of Jeroboam as well.

Interestingly, the story of the nameless man of God goes on after the
message was delivered. Jeroboam asked him to eat a meal at his house, but
he refused. Verse 9 explains, "For so it was commanded me by the word
of the LORD, saying, 'You shall eat no bread, nor drink water, nor return

---

[38] Simon DeVries notes that the context clearly points to this "man of God"
having prophetic status, and that political boundaries were irrelevant for the man
with a prophetic message. See DeVries, *1 Kings*, 170.

[39] See Lev 11:31–32; 21:1, 10–11; and Num 9:7–10 for examples of the
defiling effects of contact with the dead.

by the way which you came.'" Here we see a divine command not to eat or drink water in the area of Bethel, which amounted to a declaration of the site's impurity. Bethel had moved beyond the status of profane space to defiled space—and it had the ability to contaminate. This is reminiscent of the warnings given concerning the religious ...cs of the Canaanites.[40] The instruction to return by a different way from the original was presumably meant to protect the man of God from reprisals.[41] It might have also been making a theological statement about the contamination of the main route or "way of Bethel."[42]

What follows reinforces the depiction of Bethel's corruption. An "old prophet" went after the man of God and told him that an angel had revealed a reversal of the initial instructions. It was now permissible to eat and drink at Bethel. Verse 18 states, "He said to him, 'I also am a prophet like you, and an angel spoke to me by the word of the LORD, saying, "Bring him back with you to your house, that he may eat bread and drink water."' But he lied to him." The man of God listened to the Bethel prophet, sealing his doom. The narrative obviously makes a contrast between the man of God, who condemned the cult of Jeroboam at Bethel, and the old prophet, who condemned the man of God by deceiving him. Thus, it depicts the corruption at Bethel as extending even to the site's long-standing prophets. Ironically, the prophet from Bethel then received a true prophetic word from God, predicting the death of the Judahite for his disobedience.

Second Kings 23 reports the fulfillment of the man of God's Bethel prophecy in Josiah's efforts to purify the cult in response to the "book of the covenant" found in the temple. These included the destruction and desecration of those places where the people worshiped idolatrous gods. He was able to make reforms even in the Assyrian-held territory of the north, where

---

[40] See the discussion on Deut 12:2–4 in chapter 2. There is a similar notion found in Abraham's refusal to let Isaac marry a Canaanite woman in Gen 24:2–4.

[41] See DeVries, *1 Kings*, 170.

[42] See comments on the "way of Beersheba" above.

Bethel was located, because the Assyrian empire was in a state of decay.[43] We will limit our discussion primarily to the verses that mention Bethel—verses 4 and 15–18.

Verse 4 represents a curiosity:

> Then the king commanded Hilkiah the high priest and the priests of the second order and the doorkeepers, to bring out of the temple of the LORD all the vessels that were made for Baal, for Asherah, and for all the host of heaven; and he burned them outside Jerusalem in the fields of the Kidron, and carried their ashes to Bethel.

Purging the temple of objects dedicated to Baal and Asherah was consistent with Josiah's reform. The curious thing is that after burning all the foreign cultic elements, Josiah took the ashes to Bethel. Why? The text gives no explanation. A logical justification is the ashes of the idolatrous objects would be defiling to an altar dedicated to those gods.[44] Bethel would have been a high-profile worship site for such desecrating activity. Disposing of the ashes around Jerusalem would have had less impact on the intended audience, and the ashes certainly would not have been returned to the temple precincts. Thus, in addition to cleansing the temple in Jerusalem of idolatrous objects, Josiah defiled the major point of worship for Baal and Asherah by littering Bethel with the remains of the destroyed holy items.

---

[43] Following the death of Ashurbanipal in 626, the Assyrian Empire unraveled rather quickly, leaving a gap that the Babylonians would fill as the next ancient Near Eastern empire. The archaeological data for this period is plentiful and provides support for and elucidation of chapter 23. See Long, *1 & 2 Kings*, 509. We are concerned primarily with the text in our discussion, but the reader is encouraged to examine William G. Dever, "The Silence of the Text: An Archaeological Commentary on 2 Kings 23," in *Scripture and Other Artifacts: Essays on the Bible and Archaeology in Honor of Philip J. King*, ed. Michael D. Coogan, J. Cheryl Exum, and Lawrence E. Stager (Louisville: Westminster John Knox, 1994), 143–44.

[44] See Carl Friedrich Keil and Franz Delitzsch, *1 and 2 Kings, 1 and 2 Chronicles*, Commentary on the Old Testament, vol. 3, trans. James Martin (Peabody, MA: Hendrickson, 1996), 342.

Second Kings 23:15–18 focuses on Josiah's desecration of Bethel as an idolatrous worship site:

> Furthermore, the altar that was at Bethel and the high place which Jeroboam the son of Nebat, who made Israel sin, had made, even that altar and the high place he broke down. Then he demolished its stones, ground them to dust, and burned the Asherah. Now when Josiah turned, he saw the graves that were there on the mountain, and he sent and took the bones from the graves and burned them on the altar and defiled it according to the word of the LORD which the man of God proclaimed, who proclaimed these things. Then he said, "What is this monument that I see?" And the men of the city told him, "It is the grave of the man of God who came from Judah and proclaimed these things which you have done against the altar of Bethel." He said, "Let him alone; let no one disturb his bones." So they left his bones undisturbed with the bones of the prophet who came from Samaria.

Verse 15 traces the cultic impropriety of Bethel back to Jeroboam, linking this passage with 1 Kings 12–13. In fact, the narrator makes the sweeping statement that Jeroboam's cultic actions at Bethel actually caused Israel to sin. Josiah, by burning the cultic Asherah and tearing down the altar and high place, made the place unusable for worshiping the foreign gods.[45] Long points to the literary link between Moses and Josiah here. Like Moses ground Aaron's golden calf, Josiah ground Jeroboam's idol to dust.[46] The

---

[45] Montgomery notes that tearing down a high place is not possible, since it is a geographic feature. However, the language of the text here is metaphorical to indicate utter destruction. See Montgomery, *Books of Kings*, 534–35. For a similar conclusion to my own, see T. R. Hobbs, *2 Kings*, Word Biblical Commentary 13 (Nashville: Thomas Nelson, 1986), 336.

[46] Long, *1 & 2 Kings*, 515. See Exod 32:20; Deut 9:21. There is no mention of the calf of Jeroboam here, which may be an indicator that it was carried off as booty by the Assyrians. The theological problem of foreign worship remained and perhaps increased after the resettlement policy of the Assyrians, and that foreign or illegitimate worship is what is being addressed here. See Keil and Delitzsch, *1 and 2 Kings*, 346.

literary links between Jeroboam and Aaron are evoked as well.[47] The dust and ashes sprinkled at Bethel in verse 4 would be a defiling act. Yet the pagan gods were not nearly as strict as Yahweh when it came to places of worship. Without a change in the hearts and understanding of the people, Josiah's actions might not have prevented the people's use of the site for illegitimate worship for long.

The text does not mention legitimate worship of the God of Israel, which implies, by the time of Josiah, Bethel was an illegitimate place of worship in all respects. All association with Yahweh was forgotten or terminated, and the place was now known for the worship of Baal and Asherah. Since it was no longer an appropriate place to worship the God of Israel, Josiah made every effort to desecrate it for worship of any other god. Thus, Josiah's actions in 2 Kings 23 demonstrate that the desecration of space once considered sacred is possible.

The next references to Bethel occur in the prophetic literature. The majority of references are in Hosea and Amos, although Jeremiah and Zechariah each mention Bethel once. In Hosea, which predated Josiah's reforms by approximately three-quarters of a century, four verses mention Bethel.[48] Hosea 10 is a cry against the depravity of the northern kingdom and a prediction of its doom. The wealth and luxury that characterized the northern kingdom led to its corruption. Bethel was very much a part of this failing. One of the major forms of this corruption was the idolatry centered on the golden calf/bull located at Bethel (8:5). In 10:5, Bethel is referred to as Beth-aven: "The inhabitants of Samaria will fear for the calf of Beth-aven. Indeed, its people will mourn for it, And its idolatrous priests will cry out over it, over its glory, since it has departed from it."[49]

---

[47] Jeroboam, in addition to setting up the golden calf/bull and virtually quoting Aaron at its dedication, also apparently named his sons after the sons of Aaron.

[48] For general information on the prophet and text of Hosea, see the section on Beersheba and Gilgal above.

[49] This verse, as is the case with much of Hosea, is difficult to translate, due to the shifting between singular and plural, feminine and masculine. See the

The word *aven* (און) means "wickedness" or "iniquity." The reference to the calf indicates that Hosea had Bethel in mind; because of the calf idolatry and the syncretism it represented, the house (*beth*) of God (*El*) had been transformed into a house (*beth*) of wickedness (*aven*). This renaming clearly indicates that God was no longer associated with Bethel. The inhabitants of the northern kingdom would be distressed over the loss of their central religious symbol—the golden calf—when it was captured by the enemy.[50] Stuart has pointed to the parallel between the phrasing here and at 1 Sam 4:21–22, the loss of the ark to the Philistines.[51] In both cases, the loss of the religious symbol was equated with the glory of the god in question departing the country. Whether or not the calf was intended by Jeroboam to represent Yahweh in some way, it violated the prohibition against images, and Hosea treated it as idolatrous and central to the imminent fall of Bethel and the northern kingdom.

Bethel is mentioned again in verse 8. However, in this verse, Hosea only used his derogatory term "Aven" to refer to the site. In the context of the passage, the place in mind must be Bethel. The verse reads, "Also the high places of Aven, the sin of Israel, will be destroyed; thorn and thistle will grow on their altars; then they will say to the mountains, 'Cover us!' and to the hills, 'Fall on us!'" The high places of Bethel were equated with the sin of Israel. The text uses the plural for both "high places" and "altars," indicating that the religious activity that took place at Bethel involved the worship of multiple gods.

While Hosea alluded to Bethel's wickedness with a name change in 10:5, he went on to spell out the idea that Bethel was synonymous with wickedness itself. There can be no doubt that, in Hosea's view, Bethel no

---

discussion in McComiskey, *Hosea*, 163–67, for some more information on these difficulties. The NASB's translation is a fair treatment and I have used it here.

[50] The biblical record does not tell us when the golden calf at Bethel was captured and removed. The false worship at the site likely continued until the desecration of the worship area by Josiah. The calf was most likely carried off during one of the Assyrian invasions of the northern kingdom.

[51] Stuart, *Hosea–Jonah*, 162.

longer had any association with Yahweh. Hosea 10:15 states, "Thus He did to you, O Bethel, because of your great wickedness. At dawn, the king of Israel will be completely cut off."[52] Verse 14 is a description of sweeping destruction, including the gruesome death of women and children. Verse 15 focuses this destruction on Bethel.

Yet, Hosea remembered that it was not always this way. He recalled Bethel in a positive light in 12:4–5: "He [Jacob] wrestled with the angel and prevailed; he wept and implored His favor. At Bethel, he found Him, and there He spoke with us, even the LORD, the God of hosts, The LORD is His name."[53]

Thus, Hosea related that God's revelation at Bethel resulted in a history of communication with God there. In other words, Bethel had been a phone booth for a very long time. However, with the installation of Jeroboam's calves, Bethel lost its exclusive association with Yahweh and became associated with the Baals and other foreign deities. As a result, God refused to receive calls from there any longer. Indeed, the site became worse than profane space; it became space dedicated to evil and the archetypal reason for the doom of the northern kingdom. Enemies would carry off the calf that was worshiped there, dashing the hopes of those who placed their faith in it. From the perspective of God and his prophet, the place had become like a place of an affair that had once been sacred to a marriage, such as the place of engagement.[54] The actions of the Israelites at Bethel were a complete violation of the relationship.

---

[52] My translation. The LXX reads "house of Israel" here, instead of "Bethel." It is difficult to know which is the original reading and what text the translators of LXX had in front of them. Elliger suggests an original reading of בית־ישראל in the Hebrew text, implying that the ישר fell out. The impact on the meaning is minimal when one considers Hosea's argument that Bethel is the representative of the core problem that will bring about the destruction of the entire northern kingdom. See McComiskey, *Hosea*, 181. See also Karen H. Jobes and Moises Silva, *Invitation to the Septuagint* (Grand Rapids: Baker Academic, 2000).

[53] My translation.

[54] I am grateful to Jennifer Hearson for this analogy.

Amos shared a similar attitude toward Bethel. The first reference comes in 3:14: "For on the day that I punish Israel's transgressions, I will also punish the altars of Bethel; the horns of the altar will be cut off and they will fall to the ground." In a striking parallel to Hosea, Bethel represented a microcosm of the whole nation's problems. One of the most significant was polytheism, a practice made clear by the presence of multiple altars. The punishment for this unfaithfulness was formulated in terms of a covenant lawsuit. The picture was of the destruction of an entirely paganized place.

Bethel is mentioned again in Amos 4:4; 5:5–6; and 7:10–17. We have already touched on Amos 4:4 and 5:5–6 in our discussion of Gilgal and Beersheba. In 4:4, going to any of the sites is equated with actively sinning. According to Amos, going to Bethel was equivalent to rebellion against God. Amos 5:5–6 predicts the destruction of the sites listed. Interestingly, Amos used the term לאון to describe Bethel's fate. Hosea used this same term to describe the religious depravity of the site. The word can include both nuances, and Hosea and Amos may have been aware of the other's use of them.

Amos's final mention of Bethel is in 7:10–17. This passage is a biographical narrative that interrupts the oracles of the book. The narrative centers on the conflict between Amos and the priest Amaziah. Verses 10–13 are the most significant for our discussion:

> Then Amaziah, the priest of Bethel, sent word to Jeroboam king of Israel, saying, "Amos has conspired against you in the midst of the house of Israel; the land is unable to endure all his words. For thus Amos says, 'Jeroboam will die by the sword and Israel will certainly go from its land into exile.'" Then Amaziah said to Amos, "Go, you seer, flee away to the land of Judah and there eat bread and there do your prophesying! But no longer prophesy at Bethel, for it is a sanctuary of the king and a royal residence."

Amaziah instructed Amos not to prophesy at Bethel any longer because of its status. The translation "sanctuary of the king" can also be rendered "royal sanctuary." In other words, Amaziah was indicating that Bethel was the main sanctuary for the northern kingdom, and that it was sacred to the king. This was the reason that Amaziah gave for commanding Amos to flee from Bethel: not the power of the gods worshiped at Bethel, but its royal status. This response is not all that surprising, since Amos was there to declare the downfall of the royal family and the exile of the entire nation. Bethel was an appropriate place for this message, since it housed the worship site that represented everything that had incensed the holiness of God.

In conclusion, we turn to two remaining passages about Bethel in the prophets. Jeremiah 48:13 encapsulates the motivation for the comments of Hosea and Amos: "And Moab will be ashamed of Chemosh, as the house of Israel was ashamed of Bethel, their confidence." The comparative structure in this verse is clear. The focus is Moab, but the comparison is with Israel, which had fallen to Assyria. Moab was putting its confidence in their god, Chemosh, just as Israel put its confidence in the pagan gods of Bethel. The implication is that what happened to Israel would happen to Moab.

The last mention of Bethel is from the post-exilic period in Zechariah 7:2: "Now the town of Bethel had sent Sharezer and Regemmelech and their men to seek the favor of the LORD." This verse simply relates the fact that messengers came from Bethel to Jerusalem in order to ascertain whether they should continue their mourning for the loss of the former temple, since the new one was almost complete. It is noteworthy that there was no mention of worship at Bethel. Indeed, the fact that the messengers sought the "favor of the LORD" at Jerusalem indicates that the messengers understood that God was no longer accessible at Bethel, but that he was at Jerusalem.

Rejection and Destruction: Shiloh

While some sites, such as Bethel, were left standing even after their connection to God was broken, some sacred sites were not just disconnected but utterly destroyed. One of the most important examples is Shiloh. The loss of Shiloh's sanctity and destruction is recorded mainly in the book of Jeremiah, with one reference in the Psalms. Shiloh is perhaps the most important sacred place we have examined because of its role as a precursor to Jerusalem. Shiloh was an early spot for the tabernacle after Joshua began the conquest of the land and, initially, the place's sanctity derived largely from the ark and the tabernacle's presence there. This sanctity was later confirmed through God's revelation there to Samuel. The ark was eventually taken from Shiloh and treated as a magic item that could secure victory over the Philistines, with catastrophic consequences. The Philistines captured the ark, and Phinehas and Hophni, sons of Eli and priests at Shiloh, were killed. Upon hearing the news, Eli himself died, as did the widow of Phinehas. Apparently, after the capture of the ark, the Philistines pressed their victory and succeeded in sacking Shiloh and the worship sites there in 1050 BC.[55] Additionally, the archaeological record of the site indicates that the place suffered some destruction at the hands of the later Assyrian invasions as well. While we do not have much information beyond this about its downfall, we do know that Shiloh never fully recovered its status as a center of worship after the loss of the ark. Ultimately, Jerusalem would replace it as the primary place of communication and fellowship with God.

Later biblical writers pointed back to Shiloh's rejection and destruction as an object lesson for the people. With this in mind, we turn to the one reference to Shiloh in the book of Psalms. What interests us most is the section concerning Shiloh and the loss of the ark, in Ps 78:58–62:

> For they provoked Him with their high places and aroused His jealousy with their graven images. When God heard, He was filled with wrath and greatly abhorred Israel; so that He abandoned the dwelling place at Shiloh, the tent which He had pitched among men, and gave up His strength to captivity and His renown[56]

---

[55] See M. Haran, "Shiloh and Jerusalem: The Origin of the Priestly Tradition in the Pentateuch," *JBL* 81 (1962): 14–24.

[56] The translation follows the NASB except for this word, which I have changed. For justification of these changes, see the notes section of Marvin E. Tate, *Psalms 50–100*, Word Biblical Commentary 20, 280–84.

into the hand of the adversary. He also delivered His people to the sword, and was filled with wrath at His inheritance.[57]

The most interesting verse is 60: God abandoned the dwelling place at Shiloh. This was theological commentary on the events there. The "tent" refers to the tabernacle, while God's strength and renown are references to the ark.[58] God actively caused this destruction as punishment; the loss of the ark did not represent God's defeat. Rather, the people's faithlessness caused God to abandon his contact with them voluntarily. The resulting loss of the ark and the destruction of Shiloh presented a theological problem for Israel; these were the signs and assurances of God's presence with them. God's active abandonment of Shiloh left Israel without aid or place of assured communication. The destruction of one shrine did not guarantee that God would choose another.[59] Even such a prominent place as Shiloh was not invulnerable, because God could and did terminate this link for unfaithfulness.

Similar to its function in Psalm 78, Shiloh is utilized in the book of Jeremiah as an object lesson for the people of Judah and Jerusalem to illustrate that a place with a divine link had no guarantee of divine protection. By the time of Jeremiah, Shiloh had been defunct as a Yahwist sanctuary for many years. Furthermore, Assyria had subjected it to invasion and resettlement policies. There are three references to Shiloh in Jeremiah; in two of these, Shiloh was a foil for the temple's status as inviolate sacred space. The third reference, in 41:5, simply relates that a delegation of mourners was traveling from Shiloh to Jerusalem. This indicates that Shiloh continued to be occupied after its destruction, but without an active shrine. Of the two

---

[57] The choice of verses here was made in order to give some context to v. 60, rather than concern with the natural poetic breaks.

[58] See Ps 132:8.

[59] R. J. Clifford, "In Zion and David a New Beginning: An Interpretation of Psalm 78," *Traditions in Transformation,* ed. Baruch Halpern and Jon D. Levenson (Winona Lake, IN: Eisenbrauns, 1981), 121–41.

passages that relate Shiloh to the temple, the first is in the so-called temple sermon, 7:12–15:[60]

> "But go now to My place which was in Shiloh, where I made My name dwell previously,[61] and see what I did to it because of the wickedness of My people Israel. And now, because you have done all these things," declares the LORD, "and I spoke to you, rising up early and speaking, but you did not hear, and I called you but you did not answer, therefore, I will do to the house which is called by My name, in which you trust, and to the place which I gave you and your fathers, as I did to Shiloh. I will cast you out of My sight, as I have cast out all your brothers, all the offspring of Ephraim."

The larger context for this passage is the condemnation of the trust the people put in the temple. God used Shiloh as a bleak counterargument to this blind trust, stating that it had previously been "My place" (מקומי). As noted above, the Hebrew word often carries the connotation of "sacred place." Furthermore, in language reflective of Exod 20:24 and Deuteronomy 12, God stated that he caused his name to "dwell previously" at Shiloh. There could be no clearer acknowledgment of its former status as a sacred space. It could only serve now as an object lesson in God's freedom of choice.

The next phrase acknowledges that God was the one who destroyed what had once been his own sacred space. He specifically challenged the audience to see what he had done to Shiloh because of Israel's wickedness. Even as he caused his name to dwell there, so he destroyed the site and exiled its inhabitants. However, this passage crystallizes the idea that humanity played a greater role in the severance of the divine link than they did in its establishment. This detail is found in the all-important Hebrew word מפני; translated as "because" or "on account of," it signals the reason for

---

[60] The date for the original oration of this sermon would have been approximately 609–8 BC, during the reign of Jehoiakim.

[61] The translation follows NASB with the exception of בראשונה, which I have altered to reflect what I understand to be a reference to the beginnings of the nation prior to the acquisition of Jerusalem and the building of the temple.

God's action. God destroyed Shiloh *because* of Israel's wickedness. While there was no way to know why God chose where he would "cause His name to be remembered," there were definite reasons for the removal of his name. The other prophetic books point to the effect of the people's wickedness on God's relationship with a place, but not so directly as in this passage. God's warning through Jeremiah was that Jerusalem and the temple were no more immune to a severance of the divine-terrestrial link than Shiloh was. God was not bound to a space.

The next passage referring to Shiloh is a repetition of the message found in Jeremiah 7, but it includes the reaction of the priests, prophets, and people to that message:

> And you will say to them, "Thus says the LORD, 'If you will not listen to Me, to walk in My law which I have set before you, to listen to the words of My servants the prophets, whom I have been sending to you again and again, but you have not listened; then I will make this house like Shiloh, and this city I will make a curse to all the nations of the earth.'" The priests and the prophets and all the people heard Jeremiah speaking these words in the house of the LORD. When Jeremiah finished speaking all that the Lord had commanded him to speak to all the people, the priests and the prophets and all the people seized him, saying, "You must die! Why have you prophesied in the name of the LORD saying, 'This house will be like Shiloh and this city will be desolate, without inhabitant?'" And all the people gathered about Jeremiah in the house of the LORD. (Jer 26:4–9)

The core of this message was the same as that of chapter 7. However, there are a few differences worth noting. First, whereas in chapter 7, the former sanctity of Shiloh was mentioned, here it was not; the audience more than likely assumed it. Ultimately, it is difficult to know how closely related the message of chapter 7 is to chapter 26. Chapter 26 may be an abbreviated version of chapter 7. It was not out of character for Jeremiah, or indeed any of the prophets, to repeat their message on different occasions. Given the fuller message in chapter 7, the fact that the former sanctity of Shiloh was not mentioned here bears little exegetical insight.

Second, chapter 26 elucidates Shiloh's fate with a parallel. God states he will make the house, meaning the temple, "like Shiloh." The next phrase offers the parallel statement that clarifies this comparison. The city will become a "curse to all the nations of the earth." We are left with the following parallel structure:

For the temple to share the fate of Shiloh meant more than just destruction; it meant that it would be cursed. In other words, Shiloh went from being a sacred place, linked with God, to being a cursed place, a negative example to all nations.

The final difference is the alternate reason for the condemnation of the place. In Jeremiah 7, the reason given for the impending doom is the people's wickedness. In chapter 26, however, it is the people's refusal to listen to God's messengers. Of course, the refusal to listen should be understood as part of the more general "wickedness" mentioned in chapter 7.

The unique contribution of chapter 26 is that it lists the reactions of the "priests, prophets, and people." They were angry and seemed to perceive Jeremiah's words as a form of blasphemy. This reaction might have been, in part, because Jeremiah was preaching in the court of the Lord's house. Thus, his message was perceived, ironically, as a defilement of holy space. Interestingly, the people interpreted Jeremiah's words as meaning that the city would be "desolate and without inhabitant." This provides further clarification on what was meant by "cursed." The priests, prophets, and people were so incensed that they actually called for Jeremiah's death. Their anger was directed at his blasphemy against Jerusalem and its temple. This reveals the flaw in their thinking that the sanctity of the temple and city were inviolate—the flaw that the "word of the LORD" was attempting to correct.[62]

Both chapters indicate that the people and the leadership had come to place their faith in a place and its physical structures. In some sense, this amounted to idolatry—the sacred place became the idol, eclipsing the importance of God's presence. Underlying this conception was the notion that God needed the place, a familiar idea in the ancient Near East. Temples in Mesopotamia served as a partial residence for the god in question; the image of the god was fed, clothed, and even washed at the temple. In some fashion, the gods relied on mankind for their sustenance, a belief extending back to the creation epics.[63] Yet the biblical text always presents sacred places as the product of God's self-revelation and, consequently, as a concession to mankind, rather than a sign of God's need. These are the two ideas at war in the text of Jeremiah. In this context, Shiloh serves as the example of what resulted from believing that God needed, and thus was bound to, a sacred place.

Conclusions

The Bible tells us the reasons for God's rejection of sacred spaces were inappropriate worship and the behavior of the people; Bethel provided the most glaring example. Yet none of the places discussed above returned to normal space due to sin. It was not just a matter of the loss of the connection between God and the place in question. Unlike those places that were sacred during the moment of revelation and returned to normal space thereafter, these once-sacred spaces became cursed and destined for destruction because of God's wrath. They worsened via their association with evil, so that any attempt to worship at these sites was considered rebellion against

---

[62] See John H. Hayes, "The Tradition of Zion's Inviolability," *JBL* 82 (1963): 419–26.

[63] Mankind was created to relieve the lesser deities from the toil of serving the gods and providing for their needs.

God. Thus, places that had lost some form of ongoing sanctity became places for the faithful to avoid.

Even the legitimate sacred spaces could be corrupted through the worship of foreign deities and subsequently be rejected by God. With the loss of each legitimate sacred space, and a lack of divine revelation at new sites, centralization of worship became a practical reality. Yet, as Jer 7:12 and 14 demonstrate, not even Jerusalem—the last remaining sacred place in the land and the site of the temple—was immune to divine rejection. By the end of Jeremiah's ministry, just as he had predicted, Jerusalem was destroyed by the Babylonians.

This destruction left the people with the same tangible problem that Adam and Eve faced: extremely limited access to God. Following the destruction of Jerusalem, there was no assured way to get in touch with God. Naturally, they were not cut off completely; Ezekiel shared the image of God going with the exiles into captivity (Ezekiel 8–11). However, the problem of assured connection remained. The phone booths were all gone. The stargate was destroyed. The temple would eventually be rebuilt, giving some sense of restored lines of communication, but this temple would also be destroyed in AD 70 by the Romans. Was there a solution to the problem of a sinful people interacting with a holy God via sacred space? Was there a way to get back to what was lost in the garden of Eden with the assurance of an unbreakable fellowship with God? That is the subject of our next chapter.

CHAPTER 6

FROM SPACE
TO PERSON

The New Testament

Introduction

Before looking at New Testament ideas about God and sacred space, it is helpful to first do a bit of historical review. By the time of Jesus's ministry, the temple of Herod the Great had reached its zenith in terms of majesty and function. After the Babylonians destroyed the first temple in 586 BC, Jerusalem remained desolate for seventy years. The loss of Jerusalem and the other sacred places left people wondering how they would now communicate with God. The Jews who lived through the exile and return had experienced both the loss and restoration of the phone booth at Jerusalem. They had received reassurance from prophets like Isaiah and Ezekiel that God was still with them, even when all connections between heaven and earth seemed to be gone,[1] yet an uncertainty of assured connection with God remained. His chosen people had seen that he would cut them off due

---

[1] Both Isaiah and Ezekiel reassured the people that the exile was not the end of their relationship with God. Ezekiel relates that God actually goes with the exiles into Babylon.

to their sinfulness. As long as God remained holy and the people remained sinful, communication and fellowship remained a struggle, and loss of connection remained a real threat.

The second temple stood from approximately 516 BC until its destruction by the Romans in AD 70. This second temple was initially built by the people returning from exile, when the Medo-Persians freed them and encouraged them to go back to their homelands to start anew. Through a series of power struggles within and without Palestine, the people witnessed three changes of empire and the development of numerous factions, religious and otherwise. Indeed, much of the fragmentation of Jewish society came from efforts by various groups to ensure that a disconnect between God and his people never happened again. The various sects—Essenes, Pharisees, and Zealots, to name a few—all pointed to a desire to please God and maintain their relationship with him as a key motivating factor in their origins and goals.[2] Some groups even removed themselves from Jerusalem, viewing the temple of Herod as a place of corruption and idolatry that was still under a divinely issued edict of rejection. Others viewed Jerusalem with its new temple as the only proper point of contact with heaven, claiming that those who worshiped elsewhere were not really getting their message through to heaven. The rule of the Roman Empire over all these factions, however, was unquestionable. It was this empire and its policies that served as the backdrop for most of the New Testament writings. One main question remained: Would there ever be a secure connection with God? It is at this point that we turn the page to the New Testament, in which Jesus's life and work would change things forever, but not in the way that most expected.

When Jesus stepped onto the scene, the Jews had a functioning phone booth that connected them to heaven, but they remained under the shadow of a relatively hostile world power. The people wondered if God was really

---

[2] For more on the groups during this period, see Richard Horsley with John S. Hanson, *Bandits, Prophets, and Messiahs: Popular Movements at the Time of Jesus* (San Francisco: Harper & Row, 1985).

present. If so, why didn't he free them from the oppressive rule of foreign idolaters? Some may have wondered if their situation was similar to when the angel came from Gilgal to Bochim: God was angry at the people for failing to be faithful and would no longer support them in their efforts to be free from the oppressive foreigners (Judg 2:1). There were more questions than answers for God's people at this time, since foreign rule continued and God remained strangely silent.

Jesus as Tabernacle

Because of the advent of Jesus, a significant shift took place in the idea of sacred space and communication with God. The importance of the former sacred places faded, and the focus moved to the person of Jesus himself. As we will see, Jesus became the connection point between God and mankind.

Jesus made his debut in the chaotic environment mentioned above with a message that challenged all to think about communication with God in a radically different way. While this idea is present in all four Gospels, John is the New Testament book that contains most of the language that focuses on Jesus's relationship with sacred space. Indeed, the very first chapter of John's Gospel conscientiously forces the reader to see how Jesus relates to God's communication with man in the Old Testament.

In John 1, the Gospel links Jesus to the creation. In more ways than one, however, this link is only the beginning. The rest of John 1 is a deliberate effort to connect Jesus with the communication and fellowship between God and his people throughout the Old Testament. After the introduction of John the Baptist, in verses 9–14, we read:

> There was the true Light which, coming into the world, enlightens every man. He was in the world, and the world was made through Him, and the world did not know Him. He came to His own, and those who were His own did not receive Him. But as many as received Him, to them He gave the right to become children of God, even to those who believe in His name, who were born, not of blood

nor of the will of the flesh nor of the will of man, but of God. And
the Word became flesh, and dwelt among us, and we saw His glory,
glory as of the only begotten from the Father, full of grace and truth.

The prologue to John's Gospel is a review of the history of salvation that
started with creation, systematically highlighting key covenantal events and
linking these events with the person of Jesus.

Verse 14 reintroduces the tabernacle model. The phrase rendered "dwelt
among us" by some translations is more literally rendered "tabernacled among
us." There is little disagreement among scholars about the fact that John has
the tabernacle in mind when he states that the Word "set up a tent" among
us.[3] The word used for setting up a tent is σκηνόω, which has overtones of
the "*shekinah* glory," or the visible presence of God among the congregation
of Israel, but also includes the basic idea of "setting up a tent." John's Jewish
readers would certainly have picked up on this nuance. He thus utilized the
image of flesh as the tent in which God dwells with his covenant people. It
is fascinating to note that before the tabernacle, God's presence among the
people manifested as light veiled by a cloud. The tabernacle became the portable housing for this veiled light. John clearly intended to convey a connection between the Light, the patriarchs, the Exodus, the tabernacle, and Jesus
in the prologue to his Gospel. In doing so, John masterfully linked Jesus
with the old covenant while introducing something new at the same time.

John also presented Jesus as a new sort of tabernacle. As we saw in chapter 3, the tabernacle occupied the unique category of movable sacred space.
Wherever the tabernacle was set up, that place became sacred because God
was there and the people could communicate with him through it. Yet he
also moved along with the tabernacle. The people were not limited to one
place if they wanted to get in touch with God, because he moved with and
led them. This was the closest parallel to the idea of God walking in the
garden of Eden with Adam and Eve.

---

   [3] See, for example, Raymond E. Brown, *The Gospel according to John I–XII*
The Anchor Bible, vol. 29 (New York: Doubleday, 1966), 13.

There was an evident difference between the Old Testament tabernacle and Jesus as the new one. With the old tabernacle, even touching the items associated with God led to certain death. Indeed, Uzzah found this out when, presumably with the best intentions, he tried to stabilize the teetering ark of the covenant and was struck dead (2 Sam 6:6–7). The tabernacle and the ark were associated with God's presence, and an encounter with him was often deadly. The tabernacle was the movable link with God that carried on the Sinai encounter, wherein he told the Israelites not to come too near his presence, lest they too be struck down by his dangerous perfection. Yet Scripture paints a very different picture of Jesus. While John stated that Jesus was God "tabernacling" among his people, those who touched Jesus were not struck down. Instead, touching him often led to healing. For example, the woman with the issue of blood should have been destroyed when she came into contact with Jesus; instead, she was healed (Matt 9:20–22). John tied this thought together with the statements of verse 14. The glory (δόξα) of God was revealed in the person of Jesus. God was once again present among his people; but this time, God's presence brought healing because of Jesus's imminent sacrifice.

Jesus as Ark

John also seemed to equate Jesus with the ark of the covenant—the ark that was first housed within the tabernacle and later within the temple. The ark was the promised meeting place between God and Moses (Exod 25:22) and, therefore, the locus for the presence of God among his covenant people. For this reason, it occupied the most holy spaces within the tabernacle and temple. The ark itself had two cherubs on its top, one on either end. It is noteworthy that the word *cherub* is difficult to translate with certainty, but probably means something like "gatekeeper" or "intercessor."[4] Thus, the angels guarded access to God. The space between these angels symbolized

---

[4] J. Daniel Hays, *The Temple and the Tabernacle: A Study of God's Dwelling Places from Genesis to Revelation* (Grand Rapids: Baker, 2016), 112.

his throne. The ark was the actual telephone line that ran from the booth to God's dwelling place in heaven, and it was the closest one could get to a direct interaction with God.

So where do we see John creating a parallel between Jesus and the ark? We find it in John's account of Easter Sunday—specifically, the two angels that appeared in Jesus's tomb in 20:12. The phrasing links Jesus with the mercy seat of the ark of the covenant. Since John's prologue associated Jesus with the tabernacle, bringing a similar analogy to bear at the end of his life makes sense. In 20:12, there were two angels sitting on the slab where Jesus had been prior to his resurrection. With a different emphasis than Matthew and Mark, John specifically listed two angels present at the tomb, one at the head of the shelf and the other at the foot. As noted by Xavier Léon-Dufour, the position of the angels was very similar to the placement of the crafted cherubim in Exod 25:19, with one cherub at each end of the mercy seat.[5] Léon-Dufour acknowledges that we cannot be certain this was John's thinking in his presentation of Jesus's resurrection, but it remains a distinct possibility. Indeed, given John's love of imagery and connections with the Old Testament, the connection was more likely intended than not. The implication is that, through the death and resurrection of Jesus, all believers have access to God without the need of the ark. Indeed, Mary was looking for Jesus's body, but instead encountered the living Jesus. He was not, however, on the slab of stone, which would parallel the ark's mercy seat; instead, he stood outside the tomb and spoke to Mary directly (20:15). Because of his death and resurrection, the ark was no longer needed for communication and fellowship with God.

At the beginning of the Gospel, Jesus, in his flesh, was the Word of God dwelling among his people. But now that flesh was gone. It had been replaced by Jesus in a resurrected body. Even the intermediary element of flesh had been removed from the equation of how God's people

---

[5] Quoted in Jean Zumstein, *L'Évangile selon Jean* (13–21), Commentaire du Nouveau Testament IVb (Genève, Labor et Fides, 2007, 277n8. See also Christian Grappe, "Les Deux Anges de Jean 20,12: Signes de la présence mysterieuse du Logos (à la lumière du targum d'Ex 25,22)," in *Revue D'Histoire et de Philosophie Religieuses* 89, no. 2 (2009), 169–77.

communicated with him. Jesus was the tabernacle and the ark. Yet because of his death and resurrection, these physical elements were no longer required for communication with God. In this development, we begin to see that communication with God was moving to a greater level of intimacy than even that which Adam and Eve initially enjoyed in Eden. Direct, spiritual connection was now possible.

The book of Hebrews also examines Jesus's relationship with the tabernacle and the idea of accessibility. The book as a whole favors the use of typology to show how Jesus fulfilled the institutions of the Old Testament. In Heb 9:1–5, the author describes the way the original tabernacle functioned, noting its primary purpose was to house the presence of God in some mysterious way. Yet the author goes on to state that the intersection and interaction between God and his people were extremely limited (vv. 6–10). Not only would the high priest only enter once a year, but the sacrificial rituals for atoning for sin occurred outside the holy of holies and did not produce any lasting change in the people. Thus, according to the author of Hebrews, the tabernacle was a stopgap measure that did not really solve the problem of communication and fellowship between God and humanity. It was, at best, a moveable phone booth. However, it was limited; it could not accomplish the ultimate goal of restoring full fellowship between God and his people, dwelling together in the same space.

Hebrews goes on to describe the true tabernacle, heaven (9:11–25). In this description, instead of being the tabernacle itself, Jesus was the high priest that came from the tabernacle in heaven.[6] Marie Isaacs notes that even as the atonement for sin took place outside the holy of holies in the earthly tabernacle, so too did such atonement have to take place outside the heavenly holy of holies.[7] Since the heavenly abode as a whole is the dwelling

---

[6] It is unclear whether heaven as a whole was the tabernacle in the description of the author or if he understood it to be a structure of some sort in heaven. Either way, it does not change the meaning of the passage.

[7] Marie E. Isaacs, *Sacred Space: An Approach to the Theology of the Epistle to the Hebrews,* Journal for the Study of the New Testament: Supplement Series 73 (Sheffield: Sheffield Academic Press, 1992), 211.

place of God (Ps 11:4), it is understood to be the holy of holies, and Earth, which is the outer courts, became the place to offer the sacrifice for sin.

The Epistle of Hebrews also states that Jesus's self-sacrifice trumped the offerings of the tabernacle as a perfect sacrifice, offered once and for all. This, then, created an access to the sacred space—heaven—and eliminated the problems of both limited communication and insecurity that fellowship with God would be lost. In other words, Jesus's work as high priest in the heavenly tabernacle did away with the need for an earthly tabernacle at all (9:23–25). Heaven is the sacred space, the space where God dwells. Because of the sacrifice of Jesus and his intercessory role as high priest, all other sacred places became redundant, because their purpose has been met. Through Jesus as sacred space, sacrifice, and high priest, dwelling directly with God is possible.

Jesus as Ongoing Sacred Space

Jesus and Bethel

The New Testament also links Jesus to those sites that had an ongoing connection with God. We find several examples in the Gospel of John, with the most notable being those where Jesus himself drew the connection. Just a few verses after John linked Jesus with the tabernacle, he connected him to the sacred site of Bethel:

> The next day He purposed to go into Galilee, and He found Philip. And Jesus said to him, "Follow Me." Now Philip was from Bethsaida, of the city of Andrew and Peter. Philip found Nathanael and said to him, "We have found Him of whom Moses in the Law and *also* the Prophets wrote—Jesus of Nazareth, the son of Joseph." Nathanael said to him, "Can any good thing come out of Nazareth?" Philip said to him, "Come and see." Jesus saw Nathanael coming to Him, and said of him, "Behold, an Israelite indeed, in whom there is no deceit!" Nathanael said to Him, "How do You know me?"

Jesus answered and said to him, "Before Philip called you, when you were under the fig tree, I saw you." Nathanael answered Him, "Rabbi, You are the Son of God; You are the King of Israel." Jesus answered and said to him, "Because I said to you that I saw you under the fig tree, do you believe? You will see greater things than these." And He said to him, "Truly, truly, I say to you, you will see the heavens opened and the angels of God ascending and descending on the Son of Man." (John 1:43–51)

This story relates the addition of Nathanael to the disciples of Jesus. Verses 50 and 51 speak to the issue of Jesus's connection with sacred space. Verse 50 relays Jesus's response to Nathanael's sudden claim of belief. It is unclear why the reference to the fig tree changed Nathanael's mind about the identity of Jesus. Whatever it was, Nathanael was convinced, and yet Jesus told him (and apparently the other disciples present) that they would see greater evidence of Jesus's divinity.

The language of verse 51 is key. This evidence of Jesus's divinity would manifest in the form of the heavens being opened and the visible movement of angels between heaven and earth. There can be little doubt that this was a reference to Jacob's dream in Genesis 28.[8] As we saw in chapter 2, after the revelation in Genesis 28, Jacob realized that Bethel (house of God) was the contact point between heaven and earth. Therefore, in John 1:51, Jesus was making the claim that *he* was the contact point between heaven and earth. This association is strengthened by Jesus's connection with the tabernacle just a few verses earlier. Nathanael and the other disciples would now have their interaction with God via the person of Jesus Christ. Amazingly, John combined two of our three categories—moveable sacred space and space with ongoing sanctity—into the one person of Jesus.

---

[8] In addition to the clear allusions to Jacob's dream/vision, the fact that Jesus noted that Nathanael was an Israelite without "guile" was probably a reference to Jacob as well. Unlike Jacob, who relied on his own machinations for success, Nathanael was able to trust Jesus rather quickly.

The language of ascending and descending is utilized throughout the Gospel of John and is a key element in the theology of the book. Jesus came down from heaven, dwelt among the people, and ascended to heaven again. The text depicts Jesus as being the embodiment of both the tabernacle and Bethel. After chapter 1, it leaves the image of the tabernacle behind, instead focusing largely on the temple.[9] Yet the idea of ascending and descending remains, with particular association with the death and resurrection of Jesus.[10]

Jesus and the Temple

Jesus is not just connected with the tabernacle, however. In John 2:18–22, Jesus clearly identified himself with the temple. In some ways, this is a natural extension of the presence of the ark in both structures, but by the time of the second temple, the ark was no more. The Babylonians most likely destroyed it during their conquest of Judah in 586 BC. Ultimately, the temple at the time of Jesus's ministry had the same basic function as its predecessor: serving as a means of communication and fellowship with God.

Jesus made his temple comments in response to a challenge to his authority. He had just "cleansed" the temple in a rather violent fashion from those seeking to make a profit on the sacrifices to God (2:13–17). In response, the "Jews," as John labeled them,[11] asked Jesus what authority he had to enact such a reform. The implication of their challenge was that God alone had the authority to make changes in the religious system observed at the temple. Thus, the Jews asked for a sign that would at least identify Jesus as one having prophetic authority to speak for God. Jesus's response was

---

[9] See, for example, John 2:21.

[10] See, for example, John 3:13.

[11] "Jews" is a contentious term in modern discussion, because John used it primarily as a derogatory term. Given the contexts of the term's usage in John, it is most reasonable to understand "Jews" to mean the Jewish leaders who were specifically opposed to Jesus. However, there is undoubtedly also a sense of the general rebellion of God's people against God, since John viewed the rejection of Jesus as the rejection of God.

cryptic enough that those who challenged him, and even his own disciples, did not immediately understand his meaning. He stated that if his challengers were to tear down the temple, he would rebuild it in three days (v. 19). Naturally, the interrogators responded with a great deal of incredulousness. How could Jesus possibly hope to rebuild a structure that had taken forty-six years to reach its current state of architectural beauty in three days? John offered the solution in verse 21: "But He was speaking of the temple of His body." Jesus was equating himself with the temple.

Two elements stand out from Jesus's reply. First, his response to the Jews shows that his authority to make changes in the temple precincts was based on his own person. Jesus went beyond establishing prophetic authority to claiming the direct authority of God. This self-identification leads to the second important element. As noted above, the temple provided a link to heaven and access to God. By referring to himself as the temple, Jesus indicated that he was the presence of God among the people. In other words, he nullified the earthly temple's purpose by being present in the flesh. What is more, through his death and resurrection, Jesus yielded a means of fellowship with God that was unbreakable. Such a permanent link was not within the means of the earthly temple. Since Jesus is eternal, so too is his followers' connection with God.

In the story of the Samaritan woman at the well in John 4:19–26, we see a further development of this same idea of Jesus's identification with the temple:

The woman said to Him, "Sir, I perceive that You are a prophet. "Our fathers worshiped in this mountain, and you people say that in Jerusalem is the place where men ought to worship." Jesus said to her, "Woman, believe Me, an hour is coming when neither in this mountain nor in Jerusalem will you worship the Father. You worship what you do not know; we worship what we know, for salvation is from the Jews. But an hour is coming, and now is, when the true worshipers will worship the Father in spirit and truth; for such people the Father seeks to be His worshipers. God is spirit, and those who worship Him must worship in spirit and truth." The woman said to Him, "I know that Messiah is coming (He who is called Christ); when that One comes, He will declare all things to us." Jesus said to her, "I who speak to you am He."

This story relates Jesus's interaction with a woman who had a somewhat sordid love life. Jesus revealed his knowledge of her past, which led her to proclaim him a prophet with divine insight. While the woman did not have the same level of belief that we saw in Nathanael, her reaction to Jesus was somewhat similar. Also similar is the fact that a revelation about the changing role of sacred places followed her acknowledgment of Jesus's special status.

The woman began by declaring Jesus a prophet and then asking him the proper place for worship.[12] The ethnic group of the woman, the Samaritans, identified Mount Gerizim, near Shechem, as the proper place to worship. The Samaritans held this site as sacred on the basis that God revealed himself there to both Abraham (Gen 12:7) and Jacob (Gen 33:20). Of course, the Israelites also renewed the covenant at Shechem when they conquered the land of Canaan, which was an acknowledgment of the site's connection to heaven (Deut 11:29; 27:12). Additionally, the Samaritans believed it was on Mount Gerizim that Abraham offered Isaac to the Lord as a sacrifice, and it was where Abraham met Melchizedek.[13] On the other hand, the Jews identified Jerusalem as the proper place to worship. They viewed this as the only acceptable sanctuary, and as the legitimate place where Abraham offered Isaac. This caused additional tension between the two groups, which was compounded by the Jews' destruction of the Samaritan temple in 129 BC.[14]

---

[12] In asking this question, she was probably trying to avoid the issue of her embarrassing moral choices as well as ascertaining the level of Jesus's prophetic skill and whether he sided with the Samaritans or the Jews.

[13] See J. Macdonald, *The Theology of the Samaritans* (London: SCM Press, 1964), 327–33. See also H. L. Strack and P. Billerbeck, *Kommentar zum Neuen Testament aus Talmud und Midrasch*, 4 vols. (München, 1922–28), 1:549, 2:437.

[14] The temple had been converted into a pagan worship site by Antiochus IV Epiphanes, which was the primary reason for its destruction by the Jewish rebel John Hyrcanus, but the tension remained.

Jesus's answer was no doubt surprising to the woman. Instead of siding with the Jewish site of Jerusalem as expected, he declared that neither site would have particular significance in the dawning era. Building on the claims that he was the new access point to God and the very presence of God among the people, Jesus stated that true worshipers would worship in *spirit and truth* because of his identity. There are two main possibilities concerning the meaning behind this phrase. Leon Morris believes that spirit and truth is best understood as indicating inner attitude.[15] Raymond Brown, on the other hand, understands the phrase to refer to the Holy Spirit. He argues that spirit and truth should be understood as a single idea so that it could be read as *Spirit of truth*.[16] Though Morris's interpretation is the more widely accepted interpretation, Brown's argument makes logical sense, and it is best to count the phrase as intentionally broad in its meaning.[17] Undoubtedly, with the narrative connections between this episode and the encounter with Nathanael, there is a connection between the phrases *grace and truth* and *spirit and truth* as well. Jesus was speaking of a new element that would make contact with God possible through himself.

The Samaritan woman was concerned with knowing the proper place for assured interaction with God. In other words, where was the phone booth really located? Jesus's reply showed that he was fulfilling the function of sacred space, and therefore one's relationship with him would become the most important element for communication with God. By declaring that true worship would characterize the true worshiper, Jesus connected the past with the future. From the beginning of creation (Gen 1:2), God's Spirit was always important for proper worship. The new element would be the fact that the Spirit would no longer be self-limited to particular places. John picked up on this idea of God's Spirit working through Jesus and his followers

---

[15] Leon Morris, *The Gospel according to John*, rev. New International Commentary on the New Testament (Grand Rapids: Eerdmans, 1995), 239.

[16] Brown, *Gospel According to John*, 180.

[17] Brown's view is also supported by similar notions that the Spirit of God would purify and enable the community at Qumran to worship properly. See 1QS iv, 19–22.

throughout the Gospel, and this eventually led to the Spirit dwelling directly in the believers themselves. This, of course, is the fulfillment of Jer 31:31–34:

> "Behold, days are coming," declares the LORD, "when I will make a new covenant with the house of Israel and with the house of Judah, not like the covenant which I made with their fathers in the day I took them by the hand to bring them out of the land of Egypt, My covenant which they broke, although I was a husband to them," declares the LORD. "But this is the covenant which I will make with the house of Israel after those days," declares the LORD, "I will put My law within them and on their heart I will write it; and I will be their God, and they shall be My people. They will not teach again, each man his neighbor and each man his brother, saying, 'Know the LORD,' for they will all know Me, from the least of them to the greatest of them," declares the LORD, "for I will forgive their iniquity, and their sin I will remember no more."

As the passage illustrates, in order for the Spirit to be present in a believer, God had to change the heart and mind. By changing the sinful heart, Jesus was addressing the issue of sin that was one of the barriers to fellowship with God. As a result, believers would be able to worship God "in spirit and truth" without having to be at a particular place.

In both John 2 and 4, then, we see Jesus claiming that the role of sacred places, namely proper communication with God—whether the temple, Mt. Gerizim, or Bethel—was now being taken on by his own person. Places were losing their significance in terms of being a connection point to God because Jesus was *the* connection point; to be connected with Jesus was to be connected to God.

Further Changes to Sacred Space: The Results of Jesus's Work

While Jesus's answer to the woman at the well signaled the changing nature of sacred places, it was his death and resurrection that fully accomplished that change in a way that made God even more accessible than he was during Jesus's earthly ministry. This change became evident, first and foremost, in the tearing of the temple curtain when Jesus died on the cross. Matthew 27:51 relates this event: "And behold, the veil of the temple was torn in two from top to bottom; and the earth shook and the rocks were split." The meaning of the tear is fairly self-evident. The barrier between God and mankind, which had been present in some form since Adam and Eve were cast out of the garden, was broken. Access to God in the most intimate way was available to more than just the high priest once a year. Jesus's death had accomplished on a more widespread level what his life had accomplished to a select number.

What the disciples did not initially realize was that the death of Jesus and tearing of the barrier between God and humanity was the first step in fulfilling his promise to them. During Jesus's earthly ministry, the disciples had expressed concern about Jesus going away, since he was their "place" of access to the Father (John 14:8). Jesus initially related to them that he and the Father are one and that to know Jesus was to know the Father. One could not have a relationship with Jesus without having a relationship with the Father. Yet perceiving the concern they would have at his death, Jesus went on to reassure his disciples that he would not leave them alone and disconnected from God: "I will not leave you as orphans; I will come to you" (John 14:18). Thus, Jesus's death would not be the end, but rather a new beginning.

At first, this may seem counterintuitive. The disciples lived side-by-side with Jesus every day. They experienced unparalleled fellowship with God through him. How could that fellowship become even closer? The truth was that even their earthly relationship with Jesus had limits. The contact they had with Jesus was similar to what Adam and Eve had with God in Eden. They walked and talked with him, but also had the same barriers that people have with one another. We may love others in our lives deeply and intimately, but they are always external to us. Our thoughts and feelings are limited by words and touch. Jesus promised he would return to the disciples in his resurrected form, but this return was not the end goal. Ultimately, the Father would send the Holy Spirit (John 14:26). Jesus's disciples would be closer to God than they had been while walking with Jesus during his earthly ministry. In fact, they would be closer to God than Adam and Eve were in the garden!

The coming of the Holy Spirit to the disciples took communication with God to a new level of intimacy. No longer would God's people be limited in their fellowship with God by a place or even by external communication. God's Spirit would indwell the believers so they, like David (1 Sam 13:14), could have hearts after God's own heart. This closeness was realized when Jesus, as promised, came to the disciples after his resurrection. Jesus appeared to the confused and fearful disciples and encouraged them to be at peace (John 20:19). He then granted them the Holy Spirit in a unique way: "And when He had said this, He breathed on them and said to them, 'Receive the Holy Spirit'" (John 20:22).

Two things stand out about the manner in which Jesus gave the Spirit. First, the Spirit was given to the disciples before Jesus ascended to heaven. This means that at no time were the followers of Jesus cut off from God after Jesus returned from the dead. There was no lag time between the connection to God through Jesus and the connection via the Holy Spirit. Second, the fact that Jesus "breathed" on them was significant. This action symbolized the fact that creation was being renewed. God's Spirit hovered over the waters at the beginning of creation (Gen 1:2), and God breathed into Adam's nostrils to bring him to life (Gen 2:7). Jesus, after coming back to life, breathed this life into his followers. A close reading of the early chapters of Genesis reveals the very purpose of God's creative acts was fellowship. Indeed, the purpose of the garden and even the Sabbath was to facilitate the focus of trust and fellowship with God.[18] The gift of the Holy Spirit was a renewal of what was lost due to rebellion against God, and it increased the

---

[18] See N. Blake Hearson, "Over-Worked and Stressed Out: What Can the Sabbath Teach Us about Truly Living?" in *Coffee Shop Conversations: Evangelical Perspectives on Current Issues*, ed. Russell L. Meek and N. Blake Hearson (Eugene, OR: Wipf and Stock, 2013).

intimacy that was present in the garden. In many ways, the gift of the Spirit made communication between God and his followers better than it had ever been before.

In Acts 2, we see the spreading of the Holy Spirit to the broader church in accordance with the promise given in Joel. The prophet Joel proclaimed a day would come when the Spirit of God would be given to all his people, so they could all have the same relationship with God that characterized the prophets (Joel 2:28).[19] In other words, all the people would have direct access to God. In Acts 2, this access actualized when the Spirit came upon the faithful gathered together at Jerusalem. The focus of the passage is not on the place, but on the people and the diversity of languages. The flames above the heads of the believers (Acts 2:3) may very well have been a nod to the burning bush and the pillar of fire in Exodus, which were associated with God's communication and fellowship with the people. If this allusion is present, the fire—and therefore God's presence—was now associated with individual believers. In other words, they now had direct access to God. Indeed, many of those witnessing the gift of the Spirit in Acts 2, evident via the signs and miraculous speaking of several languages, believed, and they too received the Holy Spirit. The amazing access given to the believers, regardless of place or language, was the signal of yet one more change in the way believers communicated with God—a change whose importance cannot be overstressed. Communication with God would no longer take place occasionally at a designated phone booth. Each believer now had a cell phone with direct access to God.

The gift of the Holy Spirit changed the very status and nature of believers. Nowhere is this more evident in the Pauline literature than in 1 Cor 3:9–17:

For we are God's fellow workers; you are God's field, God's build-ing. According to the grace of God which was given to me, like a

---

[19] Prophesying, seeing visions, and dreaming dreams were all means of God's communication with and through the prophets. Thus, Joel is describing a relation-ship between the people and God that had previously only been with a select few.

wise master builder I laid a foundation, and another is building on
it. But each man must be careful how he builds on it. For no man
can lay a foundation other than the one which is laid, which is Jesus
Christ. Now if any man builds on the foundation with gold, silver,
precious stones, wood, hay, straw, each man's work will become
evident; for the day will show it because it is to be revealed with
fire, and the fire itself will test the quality of each man's work. If
any man's work which he has built on it remains, he will receive a
reward. If any man's work is burned up, he will suffer loss; but he
himself will be saved, yet so as through fire. Do you not know that
you are a temple of God and that the Spirit of God dwells in you?
If any man destroys the temple of God, God will destroy him, for
the temple of God is holy, and that is what you are.[20]

In this passage, the apostle Paul attempted to shift the focus of the
Corinthian believers away from each other and particular leaders, such as
Paul and Apollos, and onto God. In context, he was arguing that *all* believ-
ers belong to God—leaders and lay members alike.

Paul stated that the foundation of the building was the gospel of Jesus
Christ. Because of the preciousness of the foundation, the type of materials used in the superstructure was important. While the primary point of
the materials listed was their ability to endure, this certainly was not the
only meaning associated with these materials. Paul, as a Pharisee, would no
doubt have made full use of the many nuances of language.[21] The fact that
gold, silver, and precious stones were materials that would suggest the tabernacle and the temple was no coincidence.[22] In other words, Paul did not

---

[20] This passage crosses the typical pericope division by starting with v. 9
instead of v. 10. This is necessary to show the particular topic that concerns this
work.

[21] See Acts 23:6 and E. P. Sanders, *Paul and Palestinian Judaism: A Comparison
of Patterns of Religion* (Minneapolis: Fortress, 2017), and Brad H. Young, *Meet the
Rabbis: Rabbinic Thought and the Teachings of Jesus* (Peabody, MA: Hendrickson,
2007).

[22] See Exod 31:1–5; 35:30–36:1; 1 Chr 22:14, 16; 29:2; 2 Chr 3:6; Hag 2:8.

have some fabulous government building or public facility in mind; rather, he was thinking of the temple of God. Therefore, the enduring building materials that Paul cited in verse 12 anticipated the temple imagery of verses 16–17.[23]

It is noteworthy that the Corinthians would have associated Paul's imagery with their own pagan temples.[24] Paul utilized their knowledge and experience to tell them there was only one God and there could only be one true temple in Corinth. Surprisingly, this temple was not a building or even a place, but the collective community of believers in the city.[25] The holy of holies in this temple was occupied by the Spirit of God. The presence of God's Spirit and that alone marked the Corinthians as God's people and God's temple. Greek grammar indicates that the temple in verse 16 should be understood as definite—The Temple.[26] As in the Old Testament, it was God's particular presence that made a place, or in this case, a person, sacred.

There can be no doubt that calling the Corinthian church the temple of God had to be a bit of a shock to the Corinthians. Whether they thought of their own local temples to the pagan deities or the magnificent temple in Jerusalem, the comparison seemed unlikely. A group of believers living and meeting in houses could hardly have been on the same level with the beautiful structures brought to mind. While it is unlikely Paul meant to say that the Corinthians were a replacement for the temple in Jerusalem in some sort of realized metaphor from Ezekiel 40–48, he certainly intended to convey that God was in the midst of the church at Corinth. Likewise, Paul intended to warn the Corinthians that, just like the Israelites of old,

---

[23] See Gordon Fee, *The First Epistle to the Corinthians*, New International Commentary on the New Testament (Grand Rapids: Eerdmans, 1987), 140–41.

[24] See 6:9 and 8:7.

[25] The pronoun of v. 16 is the plural ἐστε indicating that the individual believers did not constitute individual temples in this context. Paul picked up on this idea again in 2 Cor 13:5, where he encouraged the Corinthians to examine themselves before coming into the holy presence of God.

[26] This is based on Colwell's Rule, the idea that predicate nouns preceding the verbal form are usually definite. See Fee, *First Epistle*, 147n11.

their behavior could have severe consequences in terms of their interaction with God. Much like Israel in the book of Judges, the greatest threat to the community of God came from insiders and not from some outside threat.[27] Even as Jeremiah warned the people the temple in Jerusalem was not inviolate, so Paul warned the Corinthians they were in great danger of judgment. Yet gone was the threat of a permanent disconnect from God. Hope remained because of the work of Jesus.

The idea the believers themselves had become the sacred space of God's temple was reiterated in Paul's letter to the Ephesians. The primary passage of interest is 2:11–22, but we will focus on 2:20–22 specifically. In 2:11–19, Paul described the previous relationship between Gentiles and Jews in terms of the covenantal program of God and described how that relationship changed because of the advent of Jesus Christ.[28] Paul used spatial terminology associated with the temple to illustrate this change in relationship. He pointed out that while the Jews had been *near* to God, the Gentiles were *far off*.

These terms *near* and *far off* refer to access to God via the tabernacle and temple. The Jews had access to God at these sacred places; in other words, they could draw "near" to God through prayer and sacrifice there. In fact, Paul was undoubtedly playing on the Hebrew term for sacrifice here: קרבן (*kōrban*). This term for a sacrifice literally means "something brought near (to God)."[29] One did not enter God's presence in the sacred place without a gift or offering. Through sacrifice and offerings, the Jews had the ability to access God's presence, whereas the Gentiles did not. As a result, the Gentiles were considered "far off" or separate from God. The idea of being near or

---

[27] More Israelites died at the hand of fellow Israelites in the book of Judges than from any foreign oppressor. See David E. Garland, *1 Corinthians*, Baker Exegetical Commentary on the New Testament (Grand Rapids: Baker Academic, 2003), 120.

[28] See Harold W. Hoehner, *Ephesians: An Exegetical Commentary* (Grand Rapids: Baker Academic, 2002), 386.

[29] This term occurs most frequently in the book of Leviticus, where there is great concern with the proper means for approaching God.

far off from God's presence was intimately linked with the idea of salvation as well. In Ps 22:19 and Isa 46:13, for example, God's presence was synonymous with his salvation; by contrast, those who were outside God's presence were, by definition, excluded from salvation.[30] However, through the new sacred space identified as the person of Jesus, both Jews and Gentiles had access to God. Thus, the distinction based on ethnic location (*near* and *far off*) ceased to be a determining factor for access to God (Eph 2:18). Both Jews and Gentiles could be included in the classification of *saints*: those who had attained a righteous standing before God through faith (2:19).

The removal of the distinction between near and far off represented a change for the Gentiles on two levels. First, the Gentiles became near instead of far off. Throughout the Old Testament, the Gentiles were foreigners in every sense of the word. They were not part of the covenant community and did not have access to God, except by joining the covenant community via the termination of their own ethnic, spiritual, and geographic identity.[31] With the shift away from geographic sacred space to access through the person of Jesus and his sacrificial blood, however, it became possible for the Gentiles to become one with the Jews, becoming part of those designated *near*. Second, the Gentiles originally had no relationship with God; now, they were reconciled to God along with the Jews. Through Jesus Christ, both Jews and Gentiles became citizens and members of God's household. Geographic proximity to places where God had revealed himself among his people was fading away, at least for a time.[32] Even as Jesus indicated to the Samaritan woman in John 4, place had become irrelevant because of the new revelation of God through the Son.

---

[30] This notion is reflected in Rev 21:1–6, 22–27 as well.

[31] Ruth was a prime example of one of the rare cases when a Gentile did join the covenant community in this way. Ruth effectively ceased to be a Moabite and became an Israelite (Ruth 1:16–17).

[32] Geography seems to play a significant role in the book of Revelation, unless one understands the New Jerusalem to be a metaphor. If physical location is significant in Revelation, then the movement from tabernacle to a more permanent place in the Old Testament is reflected in the New Testament as well.

The idea of Jews and Gentiles becoming members of one household (2:19) brings us to the three verses of particular interest. In Eph 2:20–22, we read: "Having been built on the foundation of the apostles and prophets, Christ Jesus Himself being the corner stone, in whom the whole building, being fitted together, is growing into a holy temple in the Lord, in whom you also are being built together into a dwelling of God in the Spirit." In these verses, we see that the cause of the new relationship between Jews, Gentiles, and God was the new temple in which God dwelled. There was a natural transition from the metaphor of a household (v. 19) to that of a temple (v. 20). The temple of the Lord in the Old Testament was, of course, quite literally the *house of the Lord*. As in the Old Testament, the temple in question did not limit the presence of God, but provided access to him for the people (1 Kgs 8:27).

By using the term *temple*, Paul is in agreement with the language of the Gospel of John, where Jesus compared himself to the tabernacle early in his ministry, but identified himself with the more permanent temple as well (John 1:14; 2:19). Paul moved somewhat further by focusing on the movement from Jesus as God's localized presence to believers being the localized presence, an event that Jesus forecast with the promise of the Holy Spirit (John 14:15–26). The followers of Jesus, both Jew and Gentile, made up the temple of God, in that they housed the Holy Spirit.[33] The idea here is that believers were collectively forming the new temple. Thus, believers were the new temple of God.

What was the foundation of this new temple? In the immediate sentence, there is only one definite article used for both apostles and prophets, indicating that two normally distinct groups were treated as a collective for the purpose of this passage.[34] Based on the Greek grammar, there are three

---

[33] There is some question regarding the use of the aorist passive participle ἐποικοδομηθέντες in this passage. It may be either temporal, meaning the recipients of the letter to Ephesus had already built on the foundation, or it may be causal, meaning that the reason the Ephesians were fellow citizens/saints was because they had been built on the foundation. See Hoehner, *Ephesians*, 397.

[34] See Hoehner, 397.

possible ways to translate the relationship between the apostles and prophets and the foundation.[35] The three options are "the apostles' and prophets' foundation," "the foundation laid by the apostles and prophets," and "the foundation consisting of the apostles and prophets." Given the larger context of 2:17 and 3:9–10, the second option ("the foundation laid by the apostles and prophets") makes the most logical sense. Both passages speak of the message of the gospel, and this message of hope after judgment was what the apostles and prophets had laid down.[36] The gospel, then, was that upon which the rest of the new living temple was built.

Since the message of the gospel was the foundation of God's new dwelling, Paul went on to argue that the capstone of the temple was the person of Jesus Christ. Most translations, including the NASB cited above, translate the Greek word ἀκρογωνιαῖος as *cornerstone*. This is based on the implicit reference to Isa 28:16, which spoke of the cornerstone.[37] However, first-century construction language lends itself to understanding the word as *capstone*.[38] Jesus was the pinnacle of the building, but he was also integral to the foundation, since the message of the gospel had him as its focus. The living stones that were believers were established on the good news of Jesus and grew toward the capstone of the building, which was also Jesus. Thus, the new temple consisted of the foundation and the capstone, based on the

---

[35] Respectively, the possessive genitive, the genitive of agency, and the genitive of apposition.

[36] There is some disagreement among scholars about the identity of the prophets, given their inclusion with the apostles under one definite article. For example, O'Brien argues that the prophets should be understood as the NT prophets, rather than those of the OT. Peter T. O'Brien, *The Letter to the Ephesians*, The Pillar New Testament Commentary (Grand Rapids: Eerdmans, 1999), 214. Context may very well support the idea that NT prophets were in mind, or at least included with the OT prophets. It is problematic to think that Paul, a Pharisee, would draw a sharp distinction between OT and NT prophets, but theological presuppositions differ on this point. Ultimately, assuming the foundation is indeed the message of the gospel, the division or lack thereof between the prophets of the OT and NT is largely a moot point.

[37] Note also 1 Pet 2:6.

[38] I am indebted to my colleague, Alan Tomlinson, for this observation.

work and person of Jesus, and the superstructure, made of the living stones that were believers.

Like the Corinthians, the Ephesians would have associated the idea of a temple with the temple in Jerusalem or the pagan temple of Artemis, so the idea that their small community of faith that met in homes was somehow comparable to those magnificent edifices and their privileged inner sanctums had to be virtually beyond belief. Yet Paul was stating exactly that. The temple of the new covenant and access to God was comprised of the believers through their connection to Christ. Sacred space had become sacred people. Christians were the house of God, and he dwelled within them personally and spiritually. Believers were not only able to enter God's presence freely; they were the access point to that presence. While the notion of the believer's body being the temple of the Holy Spirit and the collective body of believers being the presence of God on earth is relatively normative for modern Christians, it was an amazing change in the accepted points of access for the early followers of Jesus.

Finally, in the book of Revelation, we see the ultimate fulfillment of the role of sacred space. Speaking of the New Jerusalem in the new heaven and new earth, John stated, "I saw no temple in it, for the Lord God the Almighty and the Lamb are its temple" (Rev 21:22). God's presence will be in the midst of his people with no barrier between them. Jesus became tabernacle and temple, then granted this gift to those who believed in him and followed him. This created a level of interaction with God that was beyond what Adam and Eve enjoyed in the garden of Eden. Someday, physical presence and spiritual connection will be realized in a restored garden and renewed Jerusalem, the likes of which have never been seen before. God's people will be in fellowship with him in a setting reminiscent of the garden of Eden and Jerusalem, but better than these places' previous incarnations. Believers living in God's presence without fear or barrier will enjoy the ultimate sacred space, because all of heaven and earth will be sacred. The current state of believers, then, is one of great blessing. The hope of believers is one of greater blessing still.

EPILOGUE

Our journey through Scripture started with the nature of sacred space, its types, and, most importantly, its function. Sacred space was any place that had a connection with God on account of his self-revelation. The main purpose of sacred space was to enable communication between a holy God and his sinful people. After the fall, due to sin, communication and fellowship with God became extremely difficult (a difficulty that affected communication between people as well).

And yet, tracing the history of sacred space throughout Scripture illustrates that God always had a plan. The difficulty of interaction between God and the believer would not continue indefinitely. Whenever a phone booth was disconnected due to human sin, God always graciously provided another means of communication. Yet each of these modes of communication was limited and could be lost. With the advent of Jesus, the focus shifted from sacred spaces to the person of Christ. Through the ministry of Jesus, his followers became tabernacles and temples via the presence of the Holy Spirit. The phone booths were replaced with cell phones, as individual believers could commune with God at any place and any time and without fear of the call being dropped. What is more, the believers collectively became a single temple. At some point in the future, however, even these amazing forms of communication will cease to be, for an even more amazing reason. There will be one great family reunion of all God's people in the New Jerusalem, and all will be together with God with no distance or difficulty separating us.

If this is the case, and we as modern believers all have constant access to God, why does the history of sacred space in the Old Testament matter to us? Why should we care about the old phone booths when modern believers all have cell phones? There are two primary reasons. First of all, understanding the history of sacred space should help us realize just how amazing our current level of access is. We may have a vague awareness of the magisterial work that Jesus has accomplished in terms of the forgiveness of sin. What we do not always perceive, however, is that the level of access we have to God is part of that gift. The closest that we come to appreciating this access is feeling thankful that we no longer have to bring sacrifices. We generally tie this thankfulness to the forgiveness of sin alone, though. Our study of sacred space in Scripture shows just how difficult it is for a sinful human being to have any sort of communication or fellowship with a holy God. Yet how often do we think little to nothing of praying to God anywhere and at any time, with the assurance that our prayers will be heard in the divine throne room of heaven? Such assurance was not always present. Of course, God is omnipresent, and caution is appropriate when stating that God might not have heard someone who called out to him prior to the work of Jesus. However, the fact remains that communication was difficult because of sin, and God provided specific places and venues for worship and fellowship. Sin barred the way, and God provided grace to overcome this barrier in the form of sacred places. Our understanding of God and his graciousness is woefully inadequate if we do not understand what we have been given—and what is promised still—with respect to fellowship with him.

The second reason we need to care about sacred places throughout Scripture is that understanding how these places worked helps the modern believer to realize his or her responsibility as a living, breathing sacred place. Since the purpose of sacred spaces in the Old Testament was to enable assured communication with God, there is a similar responsibility for current followers of Jesus. In other words, our access to heaven and the presence of the Holy Spirit within us is more than just a gift for us to use for fellowship with God. It is a responsibility to the world. Israel, with her access to

God through sacred places such as Bethel, Shiloh, the tabernacle, and the temple, was to serve as a beacon to the nations. Through Israel, the nations could have some limited access to God. How much more, then, is it that believers, individually and corporately, are to provide a connection point to the lost people of the world? Too often, we take this responsibility too lightly. We tend to think of salvation as something that happens to us and go no further. We need to realize that when we believe in Jesus and become temples of the Spirit, we also become access points for those who do not yet know God. The awesome picture of our being a connection point between heaven and earth for others should flood our mind's eye. As we follow Jesus, we bear the responsibility to present him and his gospel to the world. We are not merely believers. We are, in a very real sense, sacred space that allows others to have fellowship with God.

Seeing the way God has communicated through sacred space should leave us humbled and motivated. We have access to God that Adam and Eve would envy. We have a responsibility to others that should overwhelm us. When we take stock of our place among the biblical history of sacred space, we realize just how blessed we are. Likewise, when we realize our role as a sacred place, we realize just how much the world is counting on us. May our hearts be humbled by our access to the Father and our feet be motivated by our call to carry access to him to all the world.

SELECTED BIBLIOGRAPHY

Primary Sources

Biblia Hebraica Stuttgartensia. Edited by Karl Elliger and Willhelm Rudolph, 4th rev. ed. Stuttgart: Deutsche Bibelgesellschaft, 1990.

Kantrowitz, David. *Judaic Classics Library.* New York: Davka Corporation/ Judaic Press, 1991–2001. CD-ROM.

Mechilta De Rabbi Ishmael. Edited by H. S. Horovitz and I. A. Rabin. Jerusalem: Bamberger & Wahrman, 1960.

Midrash Bereshit Rabba: Critical Edition with Notes and Commentary. Edited by J. Theodor and Chanoch Albeck. Jerusalem: Wahrmann Books, 1965.

The Midrash on the Psalms. Translated by William G. Braude. New Haven: Yale University Press, 1959.

Midrash Rabbah. Vilna: Rom, 1911.

Midrash Rabbah. Translated by H. Freedman. 10 vols. London: Soncino Press, 1983.

Midrash Tehillim. Edited by Isaac ben Samson. Jerusalem, 1991/2.

Midrash Tanhuma. Warsaw: F. Rozen, 1892.

Midrash Tanhuma. Edited by Solomon Buber. Jerusalem: Eshkol, 1971/2.

Midrasch Tannaim zum Deuteronomium. Edited by D. Hoffmann. 2 Parts. Berlin: Poppelier, 1908.

The Mishnah: Translated from the Hebrew with Introduction and Brief Explanatory Notes. Translated by Herbert Danby. Oxford: Oxford University Press, 1933.

Pesekita Rabbati: Discourses for Feasts, Fasts, and Special Sabbaths. Translated by William G. Braude. 2 vols. New Haven: Yale University Press, 1968.

Pesikta Rabbati. Edit and commentary by M. Friedmann. Wien: Selbstverlag des Herausgebers, Yosef Kaiser, 1880.

Pesiqta deRab Kahana: An Analytical Translation. Translated by Jacob Neusner. Atlanta: Scholars Press, 1987.

Pĕsikta dĕ Rab Kahăna: R. Kahanaʾs Compilation of Discourses for Sabbaths and Festal Days. Translated by William G. Braude and Israel J. Kapstein. Philadelphia: Jewish Publication Society of America, 1975.

Pesikta de Rav Kahana: According to an Oxford Manuscript with Variants from All Known Manuscripts and Genizoth Fragments and Parallel Passages with Commentary and Introduction. Edited by Bernard Mandelbaum. 2 vols. New York: The Jewish Theological Seminary of America, 1987.

Pirk̠ê de Rabbi Eliezer: According to the Text of the Manuscript Belonging to Abraham Epstein of Vienna. Translated and annotated by Gerald Frielander. New York: Hermon Press, 1970.

Shishah Sidre Mishnah. Edited by Chanoch Albeck. 6 vols. Jerusalem: Mosad Byali, 1952–58.

Sifra. Edited by Isaac H. Weiss. Vienna: Yaakov HaCohen Schlosberg, 1862.

Sifra on Leviticus: According to Vatican Manuscript Assemani 66 with Variants from other Manuscripts, Genizah Fragments, Early Editions and Quotations by Medieval Authorities and with References to Parallel Passages and Commentaries. Edited by Louis Finkelstein. New York: The Jewish Theological Seminary of America, 1989.

Sifre on Deuteronomy. Edited by Louis Finkelstein. Berlin: Hots. Ha-Agudah ha-tarbutit ha-yehudim be-Germanyah, 1917–39.

Siphre ad Deuteronomium H. S. Horovitzii schedis usis cum variis lectionibus et adnotationibus. New York: 1969.

Siphre Dʾbe Rab: Siphre ad Numeros adjecto Siphre zutta. Edited by H. S. Horozitz. Jerusalem: Wahrmann Books, 1966.

Talmud Bavli. Vilna: Rom, 1911/2.

Talmud Bavli: The Gemara: The Classic Vilna Edition, with an Annotated, Interpretive Elucidation as an Aid to Talmud Study. Elucidated by Rabbi Yosaif Asher Weiss. Edited by Rabbi Hersh Goldwurm. Schottenstein Edition, multivolume (incomplete). New York: Mesorah, 1982.

Talmud Yerushalmi. Krotoshin: David Ber Monosh, 1865/6.

The Tosefta: Translated from the Hebrew with a New Introduction. Translated by Jacob Neusner. 2 vols. Peabody, MA: Hendrickson, 2002.

Tosephta: Based on the Erfurt and Vienna Codices. Editing, parallels, and variants by M. S. Zuckermandel. Jerusalem: Bamberger & Wahrmann, 1937.

Secondary Sources

Abelson, Joshua. *The Immanence of God in Rabbinic Literature.* New York: Herman Press, 1969.

Achtemeier, Elizabeth. *Minor Prophets I.* New International Biblical Commentary. Edited by Robert L. Hubbard and Robert K. Johnson. Peabody, MA: Hendrickson, 1996.

Ackroyd, Peter R. "The Meaning of the Hebrew דוֹר Considered." *Journal of Semitic Studies* 13 (1968): 3–10.

Aharoni, Yohanan. *The Land of the Bible.* London: Burnes and Oates, 1967.

Ahlström, Gösta W. "The Travels of the Ark: A Religio-Political Composition." *Journal of Near Eastern Studies* 43:2 (1984): 141–49.

Albeck, Chanoch, and J. Theodor. *Midrash Bereshit Rabba: Critical Edition with Notes and Commentary.* Jerusalem: Wahrmann Books, 1965.

Albertz, Rainer. *A History of Israelite Religion in the Old Testament Period, Volume 1: From the Beginnings to the End of the Monarchy.* Louisville: Westminster/ John Knox, 1992.

Albright, W. F. "The Kyle Memorial Excavations at Bethel." *Bulletin of the American Schools of Oriental Research* 56 (1934): 11.

Alexander, Philip. "Midrash." In *A Dictionary of Biblical Interpretation.* Edited by R. J. Coggins and J. L. Houldin. London: SCM Press, Philadelphia: Trinity Press International, 1990.

Alexander, T. Desmond. *From Eden to the New Jerusalem: An Introduction to Biblical Theology.* Grand Rapids: Kregel, 2008.

Alexander, T. Desmond, and David W. Baker, eds. *Dictionary of the Old Testament Pentateuch.* Downers Grove, IL: InterVarsity Press, 2003.

Alt, Albrecht. *Der Gott der Väter.* Stuttgart: W. Kohlhammer, 1929.

Anderson, Gary A. *Sacrifice and Offerings in Ancient Israel: Studies in Their Social and Political Importance.* Harvard Semitic Monographs 41. Edited by Frank Moore Cross. Atlanta: Scholars Press, 1987.

Arnold, Bill T., and David B. Weisberg. "Babel und Bibel und Bias: How Anti-Semitism Distorted Friedrich Delitzsch's Scholarship." *Bible Review* 18, no. 1 (February 2002): 32–40.

———. "A Centennial Review of Friedrich Delitzsch's 'Babel und Bibel' Lectures." *Journal of Biblical Literature* 121 (2002): 441–57.

Averbeck, Richard E. "Miqdas." In *New International Dictionary of Old Testament Theology and Exegesis.* Edited by Willem A. VanGemeren. Grand Rapids: Zondervan, 2001.

———. "Tabernacle." In *Dictionary of the Old Testament Pentateuch.* Edited by T. D. Alexander and D. W. Baker. Downers Grove, IL: InterVarsity Press, 2003.

Ayad, Boulos. "The Temple of the God Yahweh in Leontopolis (Tell El-Yahudiya) East of the Nile Delta." *Coptic Church Review* 14 (Winter, 1993): 99–108.

Baker, John. "Moses and the Burning Bush." *Expository Times* 76, no. 10 (July 1965): 307–8.

Balentine, Samuel E. *The Hidden God: The Hiding of the Face of God in the Old Testament.* Oxford: Oxford University Press, 1983.

Baly, Denis. *God and History in the Old Testament: The Encounter with the Absolutely Other in Ancient Israel.* New York: Harper & Row, 1976.

Barr, James. *The Concept of Biblical Theology: An Old Testament Perspective.* Minneapolis: Fortress, 1999.

Barth, Christoph. *God with Us: A Theological Introduction to the Old Testament.* Edited by Geoffrey W. Bromiley. Grand Rapids: Eerdmans, 1991.

Basser, Herbert W. "The Development of the Pharisaic Idea of Law as a Sacred Cosmos." *Journal for the Study of Judaism in the Persian, Hellenistic and Roman Period* 16 (1985): 104–16.

Beale, G. K. *The Temple and the Church's Mission: A Biblical Theology of the Dwelling Place of God.* New Studies in Biblical Theology 17. Edited by D. A. Carson. Downers Grove, IL: InterVarsity Press, 2004.

Bechtel, Carol M., ed. *Touching the Altar: The Old Testament for Christian Worship.* Grand Rapids: Eerdmans, 2008.

Besters, A. "Le Sanctuaire Central dans Jud. 19–21." *Ephemerides theologicae Lovanienses* 41 (1965): 20–41.

Bimson, J. J. *Redating the Exodus and Conquest.* Sheffeld: JSOT Press, 1978.

Biran, Avraham. *Biblical Dan.* Jerusalem: Israel Exploration Society/Hebrew Union College, 1994.

Blenkinsopp, Joseph. "Bethel in the Neo-Babylonian Period." In *Judah and the Judeans in the Neo-Babylonian Period.* Edited by Oded Lipschits and Joseph Blenkinsopp, 93–107. Winona Lake: Eisenbrauns, 2003.

———. *Gibeon and Israel: The Role of Gibeon and the Gibeonites in the Political and Religious History of Early Israel.* Cambridge: Cambridge University Press, 1972.

————. *A History of Prophecy in Israel.* Louisville: Westminster/John Knox, 1996.

Block, Daniel I. *The Gods of the Nations: Studies in Ancient Near Eastern National Theology.* Winona Lake, IN: Eisenbrauns, 1988.

————. *Judges, Ruth.* New American Commentary 6. Nashville: B&H, 1999.

Blum, Erhard. "Noch einmal: Jakobs Traum in Bethel—Genesis 28,10–22." In *Rethinking the Foundations: Historiography in the Ancient World and in the Bible, Essays in Honor of John Van Seters.* Beihefte zur Zeitschrift für die alttestamentliche Wissenschaft. Band 294. Edited by Steven L. McKenzie and Thomas Römer. Berlin: Walter de Gruyter, 2000.

Bohak, Gideon. "CPJ III, 520: The Egyptian Reaction to Onias' Temple." *Journal for the Study of Judaism* 26 (1985): 32–41.

Bokser, Baruch M. "Approaching Sacred Space." *Harvard Theological Review* 78, no. 3–4 (1985): 279–99.

Boling, Robert G. *Joshua, A New Translation with Notes and Commentary.* The Anchor Bible 6. New York: Doubleday, 1964.

Bouillard, H. "Le categorie du sacre dans la science des religions." In *Le sacre: Etudes et recherches.* Edited by E. Castelli (Paris: 1974): 33–38.

Brichto, Herbert Chanan. "How Does God Speak in the World." Paper presented at conference called by Commission on Faith and Order of the Ohio Council of Churches, February 22, 1970.

Brueggemann, Walter. *Genesis: A Bible Commentary for Teaching and Preaching.* Atlanta: John Knox, 1982.

————. *Interpretation: First and Second Samuel.* Edited by James L. Mays. Louisville: John Knox, 1990.

Bullinger, E. W. *Figures of Speech Used in the Bible.* Grand Rapids: Baker, 1898, 1968.

Butler, Trent C. *Joshua.* Word Biblical Commentary 7. Edited by John D. Watts. Dallas: Word Books, 1984.

Campbell, Anthony F. *The Ark Narrative, 1 Samuel 4–6, 2 Samuel 6: A Form-Critical and Traditio-Historical Study.* Cambridge, MA: Society of Biblical Literature Press, 1975.

Caquot, André, "Ahiyya de Silo et Jéroboam Ier." *Semitica* 11 (1961): 17–27.

Caquot, André and Philippe De Robert. *Commentaire De L'ancien Testament: Les Livres De Samuel.* Genève: Labor et Fides, 1994.

Carmell, Aryeh. *Aiding Talmud Study.* New York: Feldheim, 1991.

Cassuto, Umberto. *A Commentary on the Book of Exodus.* Translated by Israel Abrahams. Reprint, Jerusalem: Magnes Press, 1997.

———. *A Commentary on the Book of Genesis: Part II from Noah to Abraham.* Jerusalem: Magnes Press, 1959.

Celebrating Avraham: Avraham Biran the Excavator of Dan at 90. (Reprints of articles and photographs of Avraham Biran). Washington, DC: Biblical Archaeological Society, 1999.

Childs, Brevard S. *Exodus: A Critical, Theological Commentary.* Philadelphia: Westminster Press, 1974.

———. *Introduction to the Old Testament as Scripture.* Philadelphia: Fortress, 1979.

———. *Myth and Reality in the Old Testament.* Naperville, IL: Alec R. Allension, 1960.

———. *Old Testament Theology in a Canonical Context.* Fortress, 1985.

Clements, R. E. "Baal-Berith of Shechem." *Journal of Semitic Studies* 13 (1968): 21–32.

———. *God and Temple.* Oxford: Basil Blackwell, 1965.

Clifford, R. *Deuteronomy: With an Excursus on Covenant and Law.* Old Testament Message: A Biblical-Theological Commentary. Edited by Carroll Stuhlmueller and Martin McNamara. Wilmington, DE: Michael Glazier, 1982.

———. "In Zion and David a New Beginning: An Interpretation of Psalm 78." In *Traditions in Transformation: Turning Points in Biblical Faith.* Festschrift honoring Frank Moore Cross. Edited by Baruch Halpern and Jon D. Levenson. Winona Lake: Eisenbrauns, 1981.

Clines, David J. A. "Sacred Space, Holy Places and Suchlike." In *On the Way to the Postmodern: Old Testament Essays, 1967–1998.* Vol. 2. Journal for the Study of the Old Testament Supplement Series 293. Edited by David J. A. Clines and Phillip R. Davies. Sheffield: Sheffield Academic Press, 1998.

Cogan, Mordechai. *1 Kings, A New Translation with Introduction and Commentary.* The Anchor Bible 10. New York: Doubleday, 1964.

Cohen, Shaye J. D. *From the Maccabees to the Mishnah.* Philadelphia: Westminster Press, 1987.

Cohn, Robert L. *The Shape of Sacred Space: Four Biblical Studies.* Chico, CA: American Academy of Religion/Scholars Press, 1981.

Cooper, Alan. "Biblical Studies and Jewish Studies." In *The Oxford Handbook of Jewish Studies.* Edited by Martin Goodman, with Jeremy Cohen and David Sorkin. New York: Oxford University Press, 2002.

Craigie, Peter C. *The Book of Deuteronomy*. New International Commentary on the Old Testament. Grand Rapids: Eerdmans, 1976.

Cross, Frank Moore. *Canaanite Myth and Hebrew Epic: Essays in the History of the Religion of Israel*. Harvard University Press, 1973.

———. *From Epic to Canon: History and Literature in Ancient Israel*. Baltimore: Johns Hopkins University Press, 1998.

Culler, Jonathan. *Literary Theory: A Very Short Introduction*. Oxford: Oxford University Press, 1997.

Dahood, Mitchell. "Hebrew-Ugaritic Lexicography II." *Biblica* 45 (1964): 393–412.

Davies, G. I. "Hagar, El-Hegra and the Location of Mount Sinai with an Additional Note on Reqem." *Vetus Testamentum* 22 (1972): 152–63.

de Vaux, Roland. *Ancient Israel: Its Life and Institutions*. Translated by John McHugh. Grand Rapids: Eerdmans, 1997.

———. "Arche d'alliance et tente de reunion." In *La rencontre de Diemémorial Albert Gelin*. Le Puy: Editions Xavier Mappus, 1961.

———. *The Bible and the Ancient Near East*. Translated by Damian McHugh. New York: Doubleday, 1971.

Dever, William G. "The Silence of the Text: An Archaeological Commentary on 2 Kings 23." In *Scripture and Other Artifacts: Essays on the Bible and Archaeology in Honor of Philip J. King*. Edited by Michael D. Coogan, J. Cheryl Exum, and Lawrence E. Stager. Louisville: Westminster John Knox, 1994.

———. "Theology, Philology, and Archaeology: In Pursuit of Ancient Israelite Religion." In *Sacred Time, Sacred Space: Archaeology and the Religion of Israel*. Edited by Barry M. Gittlen. Winona Lake, IN: Eisenbrauns, 2002.

DeVries, Simon J. *1 Kings*. Word Biblical Commentary 12. Dallas: Word Books, 1985.

Douglas, Mary. *Purity and Danger*. London: Routledge & K. Paul, 1966.

———. *In the Wilderness: The Doctrine of Defilement in the Book of Numbers*. Sheffield: JSOT Press, 1993.

Driver, Godfrey Rolles "The Root פרץ in Hebrew." *Journal of Theological Studies* 25, no. 98 (1924): 177–78.

Dumbrell, William J. "'In those days there was no king in Israel; every man did what was right in his own eyes.' The Purpose of the Book of Judges Reconsidered." *Journal for the Study of the Old Testament* 25 (1983): 23–33.

Durham, John I. *Exodus*. Word Biblical Commentary 3. Dallas: Word Books, 1987.

Eichrodt, Walther. *The Theology of the Old Testament*. Translated by J. A. Baker. 2 vols. Philadelphia: Westminster, 1961.

Eissfeldt, Otto. "Silo und Jerusalem." In *Supplements to Vetus Testamentum* 4 (1957): 138–47.

Eliade, Mircea. *The Sacred and the Profane: The Nature of Religion*. Translated by W. R. Trask. San Diego: Harcourt Brace, 1957, 1959, 1987.

Evans, Mary J. *New International Biblical Commentary: 1 and 2 Samuel*. Peabody, MA: Hendrickson, 2000.

Faur, Josea. "The Biblical Idea of Idolatry." *Jewish Quarterly Review* 69, no. 1 (1978): 1–15.

Fine, Steven. "From Meeting House to Sacred Realm." In *Sacred Realm: The Emergence of the Synagogue in the Ancient World*. Edited by Steven Fine. Oxford: Oxford University Press, 1996.

———. *This Holy Place: On the Sanctity of the Synagogue During the Greco-Roman Period*. Notre Dame, IN: University of Notre Dame Press, 1997.

———, ed. *Sacred Realm: The Emergence of the Synagogue in the Ancient World*. Oxford: Oxford University Press, Yeshiva University Museum, 1996.

Finkelstein, Israel, Shlomo Bunimovitz, and Zvi Lederman. *Shiloh: The Archaeology of a Biblical Site*. Monograph Series of the Institute of Archaeology. Tel Aviv: Tel Aviv University, 1993.

Fishbane, Michael. "The Sacred Center: The Symbolic Structure of the Bible." In *Texts and Responses: Studies Presented to Nahum N. Glazer on the Occasion of His Seventieth Birthday by His Students*. Edited by Michael Fishbane and Paul R. Flohr. Leiden: Brill, 1975, 6–27.

Fleming, D. E. "Mari's Large Public Tent and the Priestly Tent Sanctuary." *Vetus Testatmentum* 50 (2000): 484–98.

Frankfort, Henri. *Kingship and the Gods: A Study of Ancient Near Eastern Religion as the Integration of Society and Nature*. Chicago: University of Chicago Press, 1948.

Freedman, David Noel. "The Burning Bush." *Biblica* 50 (1969): 245–46.

Friedman, Irving. "The Sacred Space of Judaism." *Parabola* 3, no. 1 (1978): 20–23.

Friedman, R. E. "The Tabernacle in the Temple." *Biblical Archaeologist* 43 (1980): 241–48.

Fuerst, Wesley J. "Space and Place in the Old Testament." *Dialog* 19 (Summer, 1980): 193–98.

Gammie, John G. *Holiness in Israel.* Minneapolis: Fortress, 1989.

Garrett, Duane. *Rethinking Genesis: The Sources and Authorship of the First Book of the Pentateuch.* Grand Rapids: Baker, 1991.

Gerstenberger, Erhard S. *Theologies in the Old Testament.* Translated by John Bowden. Minneapolis: Fortress, 2002.

Gitten, Seymour. "The Four-Horned Altar and Sacred Space: An Archaeological Perspective." In *Sacred Time, Sacred Space: Archaeology and the Religion of Israel.* Edited by Barry M. Gittlen. Winona Lake, IN: Eisenbrauns, 2002.

Gittlen, Barry M., ed. *Sacred Time, Sacred Place: Archaeology and the Religion of Israel.* Winona Lake, IN: Eisenbrauns, 2002.

Goldin, Judah. "The Thinking of the Rabbis." *Judaism: A Quarterly Journal* 5 (1956): 3–12.

Gooding, D. W. *The Account of the Tabernacle: Translation and Textual Problems of the Greek Exodus.* Cambridge: Cambridge University Press, 1959.

Gordon, Robert P., ed. *The Place Is Too Small for Us: The Israelite Prophets in Recent Scholarship.* Sources for Biblical and Theological Study 5. Winona Lake, IN: Eisenbrauns, 1995.

Goshen-Gottstein, Moshe H. "Science of Judaism, Biblical Studies and Jewish Biblical Theology" (Hebrew). In *Studies in Biblical Exegesis: Arie Toeg In Memoriam.* Edited by Moshe H. Goshen-Gottstein and Uriel Simon. Ramat-Gan, 1980.

Goslinga, C. J. *Joshua, Judges, Ruth.* Bible Student's Commentary. Translated by Ray Togtman. Grand Rapids: Zondervan, 1927 (Dutch), 1986.

Gray, John. *I & II Kings: A Commentary.* Philadelphia: Westminster, 1970.

———. *Joshua, Judges and Ruth.* The Century Bible. London: Thomas Nelson and Sons, 1967.

Green, Arthur. "Sabbath as Temple." In *Go and Study: Essays and Studies in Honor of Alfred Jospe.* Edited by R. Jospe and Z. Fishman. Washington, DC: B'nai B'rith Hillel Foundations, 1980.

Green, William Scott. "Writing with Scripture: The Rabbinic Uses of the Hebrew Bible." In *Writing with Scripture: The Authority and Uses of the Hebrew Bible in Formative Judaism.* Edited by Jacob Neuser with William Scott Green. Minneapolis: Fortress, 1989, 7–23.

Gunkel, H. *The Legends of Genesis.* Translated by W. H. Carruth. Chicago: Open Court, 1901.

Gutmann, Joseph. "History of the Ark." *Zeitschrift für die alttestamentliche Wissenschaft* 83, no. 1 (1971): 22–30.

Halpern, Baruch. *The First Historians: The Hebrew Bible and History*. San Francisco: Harper & Row, 1988.

Halpern, Baruch, and J. D. Levenson, eds. *Traditions in Transformation: Turning Points in Biblical Faith*. Winona Lake, IN: Eisenbrauns, 1981.

Hamilton, Victor P. *Handbook on the Historical Books*. Grand Rapids: Baker Academic, 2001.

Haran, Menahem. "The Nature of the "'Ohel Mo'edh" in Pentateuchal Sources." *Journal of Semitic Studies* 5 (1960): 50–65.

———. "The Priestly Image of the Tabernacle." *Hebrew Union College Annual* 36 (1965): 50–65.

———. "Shiloh and Jerusalem: The Origin of the Priestly Tradition in the Pentateuch." *Journal of Biblical Literature* 81 (1962): 14–24.

———. *Temples and Temple Service in Ancient Israel: An Inquiry into Biblical Cult Phenomena and the Historical Setting of the Priestly School*. Winona Lake, IN: Eisenbrauns, 1995.

Harris, J. Gordon, Cheryl A. Brown, and Michael S. Moore. *Joshua, Judges, Ruth*. New International Biblical Commentary. Peabody, MA: Hendrickson, 2000.

Harrison, R. K. *Introduction to the Old Testament with a Comprehensive Review of Old Testament Studies and a Special Supplement on the Apocrypha*. Grand Rapids: Eerdmans, 1969, 1991.

Hartmann, L. "Zelt und Lade." *Zeitschrift für die alttestamentliche Wissenschaft* 37 (1917–18): 209–44.

Hasel, Gerhard. *Old Testament Theology: Basic Issues in the Current Debate*. Grand Rapids: Eerdmans, 1991.

Hayes, John H. "The Traditions of Zion's Inviolability." *Journal of Biblical Literature* 82 (1963): 419–26.

Hayes, John H., and Frederick Prussner. *Old Testament Theology: Its History and Development*. Philadelphia: Westminster/John Knox, 1985.

Heidel, Alexander. *The Babylonian Genesis*. Chicago: University of Chicago Press, 1951.

Heschel, Abraham J. *God in Search of Man: A Philosophy of Judaism*. New York: Farrar, Straus and Giroux, 1955, 1983.

Hoffman, Lawrence A., ed. *The Land of Israel: Jewish Perspectives*. South Bend, IN: University of Notre Dame Press, 1986.

Hoffmeier, James K. "Understanding Hebrew and Egyptian Military Texts: A Contextual Approach." *The Context of Scripture*. Vol. 3, *Archival Documents from the Biblical World*. Edited by William W. Hallo and K Lawson Younger. Leiden: Brill, 2002.

Hoppe, Leslie. *Joshua, Judges: With an Excursus on Charismatic Leadership in Israel*. Wilmington, DE: Michael Glazier, 1982.

Houtman, A., M. Poorthuis, and J. Schwartz, eds. *Sanctity of Time and Space in Tradition and Modernity*. Jewish and Christian Perspectives Series 1. Leiden: Brill, 1998.

Houtman, C. "What Did Jacob See at Bethel?" *Vetus Testamentum* 27 (1977): 337–51.

Hurowitz, Victor. *I Have Built You an Exalted House: Temple Building in the Bible in the Light of Mesopotamian and Northwest Semitic Writings*. Journal for the Study of the Old Testament Supplement 115. Sheffield: JSOT Press, 1992.

———. "The Form and Fate of the Tabernacle: Reflections on a Recent Proposal." *Jewish Quarterly Review* 86, nos. 1/2 (July–October 1995): 127–51.

———. "The Priestly Account of Building the Tabernacle." *Journal of the American Oriental Society* 105 (1985): 21–30.

Irwin, W. H. "Le Sanctuaire Central Israélite Avant L'éstablissement de la Monarchie." *Revue Biblique* 72 (1965): 161–84.

Jacobs, Louis. *A Jewish Theology*. West Orange, NJ: Behrman House, 1973.

Jacobsen, Thorkild. "Formative Tendencies in Mesopotamian Religion." In *Toward an Image of Tammuz and Other Essays on Mesopotamian History and Culture*. Edited by William L. Moran. Cambridge: Harvard University Press, 1970.

———. "The Mesopotamian Temple Plan and the Kititum Temple." In *Eretz Israel* 20 (Yigael Yadin Memorial Volume) (1989): 79–91.

———. *Old Babylonian Public Buildings in the Diyala Region*. Chicago: Oriental Institute of the University of Chicago, 1990.

———. The *Treasures of Darkness: A History of Mesopotamian Religion*. New Haven: Yale University Press, 1976.

Jaffee, Martin S. *Early Judaism*. Upper Saddle River, NJ: Prentice-Hall, 1997.

Jammer, M. *Concepts of Space*. Cambridge, MA: Harvard University Press, 1957.

Janzen, Waldemar. "Geography of Faith: A Christian Perspective on the Meaning of Places." *Studies in Religion/Sciences Religieuses*. Toronto: University of Toronto Press, 1973.

Japhet, Sara. *The Ideology of the Book of Chronicles and Its Place in Biblical Thought.* Frankfurt am Main/New York: Verlag Peter Lang, 1989.

———. "Some Biblical Concepts of Sacred Place." In *Sacred Space: Shrine, City, Land.* Edited by B. Z. Kedar and R. J. Z. Werblowsky. New York: New York University Press, 1998.

Jenson, Philip Peter. *Graded Holiness: A Key to the Priestly Conception of the World.* Edited by David J. A. Clines and Philip R. Davies. Sheffield: JSOT Press, 1992.

Jobes, Karen H., and Moises Silva. *Invitation to the Septuagint.* Grand Rapids: Baker Academic, 2000.

Jones, Gwilym H. *1 and 2 Kings.* New Century Bible Commentary. Edited by Ronald E. Clements. Grand Rapids: Eerdmans, 1984.

Jones, Lindsay. *The Hermeneutics of Sacred Architecture: Experience, Interpretation, and Comparison.* 2 vol. Cambridge, MA: Harvard Center for the Study of World Religions, 2000.

Kadushin, Max. *The Rabbinic Mind.* New York: Jewish Theological Seminary of America, 1952.

———. *Organic Thinking: A Study in Rabbinic Thought.* New York: Jewish Theological Seminary of America, 1938.

Kaiser, Walter C., Jr. *Toward an Old Testament Theology.* Grand Rapids: Zondervan, 1978, 1991.

Kaufmann, Yehezkel. *The Religion of Israel, from Its Beginnings to the Babylonian Exile.* Translated by Moshe Greenberg. Chicago: University of Chicago Press, 1960.

Keil, Carl Friedrich, and Franz Delitzsch. *1 and 2 Kings, 1 and 2 Chronicles.* Commentary on the Old Testament. Vol. 3. Translated by James Martin. Peabody, MA: Hendrickson, 1996. Originally published 1866–91 by T & T Clark (Edinburgh).

———. *The Pentateuch.* Commentary on the Old Testament. Vol. 2. Translated by James Martin. Peabody, MA: Hendrickson, 1996.

Kiene, Paul F. *The Tabernacle of God in the Wilderness of Sinai.* Translated by John S. Crandall. Grand Rapids: Zondervan, 1977.

Kitchen, Kenneth A. "Egypt, River of." In *New Bible Dictionary.* Edited by D. R. W. Wood and I. H. Marshall. Downers Grove: InterVarsity Press, 1996.

———. *On the Reliability of the Old Testament.* Grand Rapids: Eerdmans, 2003.

Klein, Ralph W. *1 Samuel.* Word Biblical Commentary 10. Dallas: Word Books, 1998.

Klimkeit, Hans-J. "Spatial Orientation in Mythical Thinking as Exemplified in Ancient Egypt: Considerations Toward a Geography of Religions." *History of Religions* 14 (1975): 266–81.

Kline, Meredith G. *Treaty of the Great King. The Covenant Structure of Deuteronomy: Studies and Commentary.* Grand Rapids: Eerdmans, 1963.

Knohl, Israel. *The Sanctuary of Silence.* Minneapolis: Fortress, 1995.

————. "Two Aspects of the 'Tent of Meeting.'" In *Tehillah le-Moshe: Biblical and Judaic Studies in Honor of Moshe Greenberg.* Edited by Mordechai Cogan, Barry L. Eichler, and Jeffery H. Tigay. Winona Lake, IN: Eisenbrauns, 1997.

Koenen, Klaus. *Bethel. Geschichte, Kult und Theologie.* Freiburg: Universitätsverlag; Göttingen: Vandenhoeck & Ruprecht, 2003.

Koester, Craig R. *The Dwelling of God: The Tabernacle in the Old Testament, Intertestamental Jewish Literature, and the New Testament.* Catholic Biblical Quarterly Monograph Series 22. Washington, DC: Catholic Biblical Association of America, 1989.

Köhler, Ludwig. *Old Testament Theology.* London: Lutterworth Press, 1957.

Kraus, Hans-Joachim. *Theology of the Psalms.* Translated by Keith Crim. Minneapolis: Fortress, 1992.

————. *Worship in Israel: A Cultic History of the Old Testament.* Translated by Geoffrey Buswell. Richmond, VA: John Knox, 1965.

Kunin, Seth D. *God's Place in the World: Sacred Space and Sacred Place in Judaism.* London: Cassell, 1998.

Kuntz, J. Kenneth. *The Self-Revelation of God.* Philadelphia: Westminster, 1967.

Kutsko, John F. *Between Heaven and Earth: Divine Presence and Absence in the Book of Ezekiel.* Winona Lake, IN: Eisenbrauns, 2000.

LaRocca-Pitts, Elizabeth C. *"Of Wood and Stone": The Significance of Israelite Cultic Items in the Bible and Its Early Interpreters.* Harvard Semitic Monographs 61. Edited by Peter Machinist. Winona Lake, IN: Eisenbrauns, 2001.

Levenson, Jon D. "From Temple to Synagogue: 1 Kings 8." In *Traditions in Transformation: Turning Points in Biblical Faith.* Edited by Baruch Halpern and Jon D. Levenson. Winona Lake, IN: Eisenbrauns, 1981.

————. *The Hebrew Bible, The Old Testament, and Historical Criticism: Jews and Christians in Biblical Studies.* Louisville, KY: Westminster/John Knox, 1993.

Levine, Baruch A. *In the Presence of the Lord: A Study of Cult and Some Cultic Terms in Ancient Israel.* Leiden: Brill, 1974.

————. "The Language of Holiness: Perceptions of the Sacred in the Hebrew Bible." In *Backgrounds for the Bible*. Edited by Michael P. O'Conner and David Noel Freedman. Winona Lake, IN: Eisenbrauns, 1987.

————. *Introduction to Leviticus: The Traditional Hebrew Text with a New JPS Translation*, xi–xli. Philadelphia: Jewish Publication Society, 1989.

————. "The Next Phase in Jewish Religion: The Land of Israel as Sacred Space." In *Tehillah le-Moshe: Biblical and Judaic Studies in Honor of Moshe Greenberg*. Edited by Mordechai Cogan, Barry L. Eichler, and Jeffery H. Tigay, 245–57. Winona Lake, IN: Eisenbrauns, 1997.

————. *Numbers 1–20: A New Translation with Introduction and Commentary*. Anchor Bible Series 4. New York: Doubleday, 1993.

————. *Numbers 21–36: A New Translation with Introduction and Commentary*. Anchor Bible Series 5. New York: Doubleday, 2000.

————. "On the Presence of God in Biblical Religion." In *Religions in Antiquity: Essays in Honor of Erwin Ramsdell Goodenough*. Edited by J. Neusner, 71–87. Leiden: E. J. Brill, 1968.

Levine, Lee I. *The Ancient Synagogue: The First Thousand Years*. New Haven: Yale University Press, 2000.

Levinson, Bernard. "McConville's Law and Theology in Deuteronomy." *Jewish Quarterly Review* 80 (1990): 396–404.

Lipschits, Oded, and J. Blenkinsopp, eds. *Judah and the Judeans in the Neo-Babylonian Period*. Winona Lake, IN: Eisenbrauns, 2003.

Long, Jesse C., Jr. *1 & 2 Kings*. College Press NIV Commentary. Edited by Terry Briley and Paul Kissling. Joplin, MO: College Press, 2002.

Luckenbill, D. D. *The Annals of Sennacherib*. Chicago: University of Chicago Press, 1924.

Lust, J. "A Gentle Breeze or a Roaring Thunderous Sound?" *Vetus Testamentum* 25 (1975): 110–15.

Malamat, Abraham. "The Sacred Sea." In *Sacred Space: Shrine, City, Land*. Edited by B. Z. Kedar and R. J. Z. Werblowsky. New York: New York University Press, 1998.

Marmorstein, Arthur. *Studies in Jewish Theology*. London: Oxford University Press, 1950.

Martens, Elmer A. *God's Design: A Focus on Old Testament Theology*. Grand Rapids: Baker, 1994.

————. "The Multicolored Landscape of Old Testament Theology." In *The Flowering of Old Testament Theology: A Reader in Twentieth-Century Old*

Testament Theology, 1930–1990. Edited by B. C. Ollenburger, E. A. Martens, and G. F. Hasel. Winona Lake, IN: Eisenbrauns, 1992.

———. "Land and Lifestyle." In *The Flowering of Old Testament Theology: A Reader in Twentieth-Century Old Testament Theology, 1930–1990*. Edited by B. C. Ollenburger, E. A. Martens, and G. F. Hasel. Winona Lake, IN: Eisenbrauns, 1992.

Martin, James D. *The Book of Judges*. Cambridge: Cambridge University Press, 1975.

Matthews, Victor H. "Physical Space, Imagined Space, and 'Lived Space' in Ancient Israel." *Biblical Theology Bulletin* 33, no. 1 (2003): 12–20.

Mauchline, John. *1 and 2 Samuel*. New Century Bible. London: Oliphants, 1971.

Mayes, A. D. H. *New Century Bible: Deuteronomy*. Greenwood, SC: Attic Press, 1979.

Mays, James Luther. *Hosea: A Commentary*. Philadelphia: Westminster, 1969.

McCarter, P. Kyle. *I Samuel: A New Translation with Introduction Notes and Commentary*. 8, The Anchor Bible. New York: Doubleday, 1980.

McComiskey, Thomas Edward, ed. *The Minor Prophets: An Exegetical and Expository Commentary*. 3 vols. Grand Rapids: Baker, 1992.

McConville, J. G. "1 Kings VIII 46–53 and the Deuteronomic Hope." *Vetus Testamentum* XLII, no. 1 (1992): 67–79.

———. *Grace in the End: A Study in Deuteronomic Theology*. Grand Rapids: Zondervan, 1993.

———. *Judgment and Promise: An Interpretation of the Book of Jeremiah*. Winona Lake, IN: Eisenbrauns, 1993.

———. *Law and Theology in Deuteronomy*. Sheffield: JSOT Press, 1998.

McConville, J. G., and J. G. Millars. *Time and Place in Deuteronomy*. JSOT Supplemental Series 179. Sheffield: Sheffield Academic Press, 1994.

Mendels, Doron. "The Temple in the Hellenistic Period and in Judaism." In *Sacred Space: Shrine, City, Land*. Edited by B. Z. Kedar and R. J. Z. Werblowsky. New York: New York University Press, 1998.

Mihaly, Eugene. "A Rabbinic Defense of the Election of Israel: An Analysis of Sifre Deuteronomy 32, 9, Pisqa 312." *HUCA* 35 (1964), 103–44.

Miles, Jack. *God: A Biography*. New York: Alfred A. Knopf, 1995.

Milgrom, Jacob. *Leviticus: A New Translation with Introduction and Commentary*. Anchor Bible Series 3. New York: Doubleday, 1991.

———. "The Shared Custody of the Tabernacle and a Hittite Analogy." *Journal of the American Oriental Society* 90 (1970): 204–9.

Montgomery, James A. *A Critical and Exegetical Commentary on The Books of Kings*. International Critical Commentary. Translated by Henry Snyder Gehman. Edinburgh: T&T Clark, 1967.

Morgenstern, Julian. *The Ark, The Ephod, and The Tent of Meeting*. Vol. 2, Henry and Ida Krolik Memorial Publications. Cincinnati: Hebrew Union College Press, 1945.

———. *The Book of Genesis: A Jewish Perspective*. New York: Schocken Books, 1965.

Morris, Leon. *The Gospel according to John*. Rev. New International Commentary on the New Testament. Grand Rapids: Eerdmans, 1995, 239.

Negev, Avraham, ed. *Archaeological Encyclopedia of the Holy Land*. Englewood, NJ: SBS, 1980.

Neuberg, Frank J. "An Unrecognized Meaning of Hebrew *DOR*." *Journal of Near Eastern Studies* 9, no. 4 (1950): 215–17.

Neusner, Jacob. *Rabbinic Judaism: Structure and System*. Minneapolis: Fortress, 1995.

———. *The Halakhah: Inside the Walls of the Israelite Household at the Meeting of Time and Space*. Leiden: Brill, 2000.

———. *The Idea of Purity in Ancient Judaism*. Leiden: Brill, 1973.

———. "Map Is Without Territory: Mishnah's System of Sacrifice and Sanctuary." *History of Religions* 19 (1979): 103–27.

Nicholson, Ernest. "The Centralization of the Cult in Deuteronomy." *Vetus Testamentum* 13 (1963): 380–89.

Niehaus, Jeffrey J. *Amos*. In vol. 1 of *The Minor Prophets: An Exegetical and Expository Commentary*. Edited by Thomas Edward McComiskey. Grand Rapids: Baker, 1992.

———. "The Central Sanctuary: Where and When?" *Tyndale Bulletin* 43, no. 1 (May 1992): 3–30.

———. *God at Sinai: Covenant and Theophany in the Bible and Ancient Near East*. Grand Rapids: Zondervan, 1995.

———. "In the Wind of the Storm: Another Look at Genesis iii 8." *Vetus Testamentum* 44, no. 2 (April 1994): 263–67.

———. "Theophany." In *New International Dictionary of Old Testament Theology and Exegesis*, 5:1247–50. Grand Rapids: Zondervan, 1997, 2001.

Noth, Martin. *The Deuteronomistic History*. Edited by David J. A. Clines, Philip R. Davies, and David M. Gunn. Translated by J. Doull et al. Journal for the Study of the Old Testament Supplement 15. Sheffield: University of Sheffield Press, 1981.

———. *The History of Israel.* Translated by P. R. Ackroyd. London: A & C Black, 1960.

———. *A History of Pentateuchal Tradition.* Translated by Helen Lederer. Cincinnati: Hebrew Union College Press, 1966.

———. "Samuel und Silo." *Vetus Testamentum* 13 (1963): 390–400.

Oesterley, William Oscar Emil. "The Burning Bush." *Expository Times* 18, no. 11 (August 1907): 510–12.

Oppenheim, A. Leo. *Ancient Mesopotamia: Portrait of a Dead Civilization.* Chicago: University of Chicago Press, 1977.

———, et al., eds. *Assyrian Dictionary of the Oriental Institute of the University of Chicago.* Chicago: Oriental Institute of the University of Chicago, 1956–2011.

Otto, Eckart. *Jakob in Sichem: überlieferungsgeschichtle, archäologische und territorialeschichtle Studien zur Entstehungsgeschichte Israels.* Stuttgart: Kohlhammer, 1979.

Otto, Rudolph. *The Idea of the Holy: An inquiry into the Non-rational factor in the idea of the divine and its relation to the rational.* Translated by John W. Harvey. London: Oxford University Press, 1958.

Pagolu, A. *The Religion of the Patriarchs.* Sheffield: JSOT Press, 1998.

Pahl, Jon. *Shopping Malls and Other Sacred Spaces: Putting God in Place.* Grand Rapids: Brazos, 2003.

Palmer, A. Smythe. *Jacob at Bethel: The Vision—The Stone—The Anointing. An Essay in Comparative Religion.* London: David Nutt, 1899.

Parente, Fausto. "Onias III' Death and the Founding of the Temple of Leontopolis." In *Josephus and the History of the Greco-Roman Period: Essays in Memory of Morton Smith.* Edited by F. Parente and J. Sievers. Leiden: Brill, 1994.

Pearce, R. A. "Shiloh and Jeremiah VII 12, 14 & 15." *Vetus Testamentum* 23 (1973): 105–8.

Perrin, Nicholas. *Jesus the Temple.* Grand Rapids: Baker Academic, 2010.

Pfeiffer, Henrik. *Das Heiligtum von Bethel im Spiegel des Hoseabuches.* Göttingen: Vandenhoeck & Ruprecht, 1999.

Rapp, Hans A. *Jakob in Bet-El: Gen 35,1–15 und die Jüdische Literatur des 3. und 2. Jahrhunderts.* Herders Biblische Studien Band 29. Herausgegeben von Hans-Josef Klauck und Erich Zenger. Freiburg: Herder, 2001.

Rendtorff, Rolf. *Canon and Theology: Overtures to an Old Testament Theology.* Translated by Margaret Kohl. Minneapolis: Fortress, 1993.

Rice, Gene. *Nations under God: A Commentary on the Book of 1 Kings.* Grand Rapids: Eerdmans, 1990.

Richter, Sandra L. *The Deuteronomistic History and the Name Theology*. New York: Walter de Gruyter, 2002.

Robinson, J. *The First Book of Kings*. Cambridge: Cambridge University Press, 1972.

Rowland, Christopher. "John 1.51, Jewish Apocalyptic and Targumic Tradition." *New Testament Studies* 30 (1984): 498–507.

Sailhamer, John H. "Biblical Theology and the Composition of the Hebrew Bible." In *Biblical Theology: Retrospect and Prospect*. Edited by Scott J. Hafemann. Downers Grove, IL: InterVarsity Press, 2002.

Sanders, E. P. *Judaism: Practice and Belief, 63 BCE–66 CE*. London: SCM Press, 1992.

Sarason, Richard S. "Interpreting Rabbinic Biblical Interpretation: The Problem of Midrash, Again." In *Hesed ve-Emet: Studies in Honor of Ernst S. Frerichs*, edited by Jodi Magness and Seymour Gitin, 133–54. Atlanta: Scholars, 1998.

Sarna, Nahum M. "Genesis 21:33: A Study in the Development of a Biblical Text and Its Rabbinic Transformation." In *From Ancient Israel to Modern Judaism: Intellect in Quest of Understanding: Essays in Honor of Marvin Fox*. Edited by J. Neusner, E. S. Frerichs, and N. M. Sarna, 1:69–75. 4 vols. Atlanta: Scholars, 1989.

———. *Exodus*. Jewish Publication Society Torah Commentary. Skokie, IL: Varda Books, 2004.

———. *Understanding Genesis*. New York: McGraw-Hill, 1966.

Sasson, Jack M. "The Lord of Hosts, Seated over the Cherubs." In *Rethinking the Foundations: Historiography in the Ancient World and in the Bible, Essays in Honor of John Van Seters*. Edited by Steven L. McKenzie and Thomas Römer. Berlin: Walter de Gruyter, 2000.

Schechter, Solomon. *Some Aspects of Rabbinic Theology*. New York: Macmillan, 1909.

Schley, Donald G. *Shiloh: A Biblical City in Tradition and History*. Journal for the Study of Old Testament Supplement 63. Edited by David J. A. Clines and Philip R. Davies. Sheffield: JSOT Press, 1989.

Schwartz, Glenn M. "Pastoral Nomadism in Ancient Western Asia." In *Civilizations of the Ancient Near East*. Edited by Jack M. Sasson et al. New York: Scribner and Sons, 1995.

Schwartz, Joshua. *Sanctity of Time and Space in Tradition and Modernity*. Leiden: Brill, 1998.

Scott, Robert B. Y. "Meteorological Phenomena and Terminology in the Old Testament." *Zeitschrift für die alttestamentliche Wissenschaft* 64, no. 1 (1952): 11–25.

Seltzer, Robert M. *Aspects of Biblical Thought.* New York: Joint Commission on Jewish Education of the UAHC and the CCAR, 1966.

Shapiro, David S. "The Ideological Foundations of the Halakhah." *Tradition* 9 (1967): 100–22.

Shiner, Larry E. "Sacred Space, Profane Space, Human Space." *Journal of the American Academy of Religion* 40, no. 4 (December 1972): 425–36.

Sievers, Joseph. "'Where Two or Three . . .' : The Rabbinic Concept of Shekhinah and Matthew 18,20." In *Standing before God: Studies on Prayer in Scripture and in Tradition, with Essays.* Edited by A. Finkel and L. Frizzell. New York: Ktav, 1981.

Simons, J. *Geographical and Topographical Texts of the Old Testament.* Leiden: Brill, 1959.

Singer, Itmar. "A City of Many Temples: Hattusa, Capital of Hittites." In *Sacred Space: Shrine, City, Land.* Edited by B. Z. Kedar and R. J. Z. Werblowsky. New York: New York University Press, 1998.

Skipwith, G. H. "The Burning Bush and the Garden of Eden: A Study in Comparative Mythology." *Jewish Quarterly Review* 10, no. 3 (April 1898): 489–502.

Smart, James D. *The Past, Present, and Future of Biblical Theology.* Philadelphia: Westminster, 1979.

Smith, Jonathan Z. "Earth and Gods." *Journal of Religion* 49 (1969): 103–27.

———. *Map Is Not Territory: Studies in the History of Religion.* Studies in Judaism in Late Antiquity 23. Leiden: Brill, 1978.

———. "Religion Up and Down, Out and In." In *Sacred Time, Sacred Space: Archaeology and the Religion of Israel.* Edited by Barry M. Gittlen. Winona Lake, IN: Eisenbrauns, 2002.

———. *To Take Place: Toward Theory in Ritual.* Chicago: University of Chicago Press, 1987.

Smith, Mark S. "Matters of Space and Time in Exodus and Numbers." In *Theological Exegesis: Essays in Honor of Brevard S. Childs.* Edited by C. Seitz and K. Greene-McCreight. Grand Rapids: Eerdmans, 1999.

Soggin, J. Alberto. *Joshua: A Commentary.* Translated by John Bowden. Philadelphia: Westminster, 1972.

————. *Judges: A Commentary.* Translated by John Bowden. Philadelphia: Westminster, 1981.

Stuart, Douglas. *Hosea-Jonah.* Word Biblical Commentary 31. Dallas: Word Books, 1987.

Tate, Marvin E. *Psalms 51–100.* Word Biblical Commentary 20. Dallas: Word Books, 1990.

Taylor, Joan E. "A Second Temple in Egypt: The Evidence for the Zadokite Temple of Onias." *Journal for the the Study of Judaism* 29 (1998): 297–321.

Terrien, Samuel L. *The Elusive Presence: The Heart of Biblical Theology.* San Francisco: Harper and Row, 1978.

————. "Presence in Absence." In *The Flowering of Old Testament Theology: A Reader in Twentieth-Century Old Testament Theology, 1930–1990.* Edited by B. C. Ollenburger, E. A. Martens, and G. F. Hasel. Winona Lake, IN: Eisenbrauns, 1992.

Theodor, Julius. *Midrash Bereschit Rabbah.* 3 vols. Berlin: Bi-defus Tsevi Hirsh, 1912–29.

Tomes, Roger. "Our Holy and Beautiful House: When and Why Was 1 Kings 6–8 Written?" *Journal for the Study of the Old Testament* 70 (1996): 33–50.

Tsevat, M. "Theology of the Old Testament—A Jewish View." *Horizons in Biblical Theology* 8 (1986): 33–50.

Turner, H. *From Temple to Meeting House: The Phenomenology and Theology of Places of Worship.* The Hague: Motion, 1979.

Turner, Victor. "The Center Out There: The Pilgrim's Goal." *History of Religions* 12 (1973): 211–15.

Urbach, Ephraim E. *The Sages: Their Concepts and Beliefs.* Translated by Israel Abrahams. Jerusalem: Magnes Press, Hebrew University, 1975.

Van der Leeuw, Gerardus. *Religion in Essence and Manifestation: A Study in Phenomenology.* Translated by John E. Turner. London: George Allen & Unwin. 1938.

Van Seters, John. *Abraham in History and Tradition.* New Haven: Yale University Press, 1975.

————. "The Pentateuch." In *The Hebrew Bible Today: An Introduction to Critical Issues.* Edited by Steven L. McKenzie and M. Patrick Graham. Louisville: Westminster John Knox, 1998.

Vatsyayan, K., ed. *Concepts of Space: Ancient and Modern.* Abhinav, 1991.

Vaughan, Patrick H. *The Meaning of BĀMÂ in the Old Testament: A Study of Etymological, Textual, and Archaeological Evidence.* Cambridge: Cambridge University Press, 1974.

von Rad, Gerhard. *Deuteronomium-Studien.* Göttingen: Vandenhoeck & Ruprecht, 1947.

———. *Genesis: A Commentary.* Philadelphia: Westminster, 1972.

———. *Deuteronomy, A Commentary.* Old Testament Library. Philadelphia: Westminster, 1966.

———. *Old Testament Theology.* 2 vols. Translated by D. M. G. Stalker. New York: Harper & Row, 1962.

Vos, Geerhardus. *Biblical Theology: Old and New Testaments.* Grand Rapids: Eerdmans, 1948.

Vriezen, Theodorus C. "The Nature of the Knowledge of God." In *The Flowering of Old Testament Theology: A Reader in Twentieth-Century Old Testament Theology, 1930–1990.* Edited by B. C. Ollenburger, E. A. Martens, and G. F. Hasel. Winona Lake, IN: Eisenbrauns, 1992.

Waltke, Bruce. *Genesis: A Commentary.* Grand Rapids: Zondervan, 2001.

Waltke, Bruce K., and M. O'Conner. *An Introduction to Hebrew Syntax.* Winona Lake, IN: Eisenbrauns, 1990.

Walton, John H. *Genesis.* NIV Application Commentary. Grand Rapids: Zondervan, 2001.

Walton, Kevin. *Thou Traveller Unknown: The Presence and Absence of God in the Jacob Narrative.* Waynesboro, GA: Paternoster, 2003.

Weinfeld, Moshe. "Cult Centralization in Israel in the Light of a Neo-Babylonian Analogy." *Journal of Near Eastern Studies* 23 (1964): 202–12.

———. *Deuteronomy and the Deuteronomic School.* Winona Lake, IN: Eisenbrauns, 1992.

———. "Presence, Divine." In vol. 13, *Encyclopedia Judaica.* Jerusalem: Keter, 1971.

Weisberg, David. "A Neo-Babylonian Temple Report." *Journal of the American Oriental Society* 87 (1967): 8–12.

Weisman, Z. "National Consciousness in the Patriarchal Promises." *Journal for the Study of the Old Testament* 31 (1985): 55–73.

Wellhausen, Julius. *Die Composition des Hexateuchs und der historischen Bücher des Alten Testaments.* Berlin: Georg Reimer, 1899.

————. *Prolegomena to the History of Ancient Israel.* New York: Meridian, 1957. Reprint of *Prolegomena to the History of Israel.* Translated by J. Sutherland Black and Allen Menzies, with preface by W. Robertson Smith. Edinburgh: Adam & Charles Black, 1885. Translation of *Prolegomena zur Geschichte Israels.* 2d ed. Berlin: G. Reimer, 1883.

Wenham, Gordon J. "Deuteronomy and the Central Sanctuary." *Tyndale Bulletin* 22 (1971): 103–18.

————. *Exploring the Old Testament: A Guide to the Pentateuch.* Exploring the Bible Series 1. Downers Grove, IL: InterVarsity Press, 2003.

————. *Story as Torah: Reading the Old Testament Narrative Ethically.* Grand Rapids: Baker Academic, 2000.

————. *Genesis 16–50.* Word Biblical Commentary 2. Dallas: Word Books, 1994.

Wilcoxen, Jay A. "Political Background of Jeremiah's Temple Sermon." In *Scripture in History and Theology,* 151–66. Pittsburgh Theological Monograph Series 17. Pittsburgh: Pickwick, 1977.

Williams, Jay G. "The Structure of Judges 2.6–16.31." *Journal for the Study of the Old Testament* 49 (1991): 77–85.

Willis, John T. *First and Second Samuel.* Living Word Commentary on the Old Testament. Austin, TX: Sweet, 1982.

Wolff, Katherine Elena. *»Geh in das Land, das ich Dir zeigen werde . . .« Das Land Israel in der frühen rabbinischen Tradition und im Neuen Testament.* Reihe 23 Europäische Hochschulschriften, Band 340. Frankfurt am Main: Peter Lang, 1989.

Woudstra, Marten H. *The Ark of the Covenant from Conquest to Kingship.* Philadelphia: Presbyterian and Reformed, 1965.

Wright, G. Ernest. *The Rule of God: Essays in Biblical Theology.* Garden City, NJ: Doubleday, 1960.

————. *Shechem: The Biography of a Biblical City.* London: Gerald Duckworth, 1965.

Wyk, W. C. van. "The Translation of *mqwm* ('land') in the Temple Speech of Jeremiah." *Ou-Testamentiese Werkgemeenskap in Suider Africa* 24 (1981–82): 103–9.

Young, Brad H. *Jesus the Jewish Theologian.* Peabody, MA: Hendrickson, 1995.

Zevit, Ziony. "Philology and Archaeology: Imagining New Questions, Begetting New Ideas." In *Sacred Time, Sacred Space: Archaeology and the Religion of Israel.* Edited by Barry M. Gittlen. Winona Lake, IN: Eisenbrauns, 2002.

———. *The Religions of Ancient Israel: A Synthesis of Parallactic Approaches.* London: Continuum, 2001.

Zohary, Michael. *Plants of the Bible: A Complete Handbook of All the Plants with 200 full-color plates taken in the natural habitat.* London: Cambridge University Press, 1962.

NAME AND SUBJECT INDEX

P

Palmer, Abram Smythe, 61
Parallelism, 32
Paul, as Pharisee, 128–29
Pentecost, 127
Phone booth, xviii, 3–4, 7–8, 13–14, 17,
    19, 33, 57–59, 74, 81, 86, 100, 109,
    111–12, 117, 123, 127, 135–36
Pillar of fire, 127
"Place," Hebrew noun, 32, 58, 105
Polytheism, sin of Israel, 101
Priests, Shiloh, 75–77
Promised Land, 12, 18–20, 57, 68, 73
Psalms, Shiloh in the, 102–4

R

Rejection
    Bethel, 90–102
    Gilgal and Beersheba, 82–90
    Shiloh, 102–8
"To remember," Hebrew verb, 16–17
Resurrection, importance of, 124
Revelation
    book of, 134
    dearth of, 77
Richter, Sandra L., 23, 28, 33
Ringgren, Helmer, 18
Robinson, J., 28, 30–31, 36
Ruth, Moabite, 131

S

Sacred space, xviii, 1, 4, 11–15, 22–24,
    29, 32–34, 36, 39, 41, 43–47,
    49–55, 57, 59, 61, 63–67, 69–71,
    79–81, 86, 93, 104–5, 108–9, 111,
    113–14, 117–19, 123–24, 130–31,
    134–37
Sacrifice, pagan, 85
Samaria, 88
Samaritan temple, 122
Samson, 46
Sanctified person, 45
Sanders, E. P., 128
Sarason, Richard, xii, 9, 16, 62–63, 85
Sarna, Nahum M., 42, 58–60, 63

Saul, King, 82, 84, 90
Scharbert, Josef, 18
Schley, Donald G., 75
Second Temple Judaism, sects of, 112
September 11, 1
Septuagint, 25–26, 100
Seters, John Van, 23
Shechem, importance of, 122–24
Shiloh, xvii, 8, 13–14, 75–81, 90,
    102–8
Silva, Moises, 100
Sin, 5, 7, 16, 86–88, 91, 97, 99, 101,
    108–9, 112, 117–18, 124, 135–36
Sinai, xvii, 15–16
Sinai/Horeb, 42
Skipwith, G. H., 43
Soggin, J. Alberto, 72
Solomon, prayer of, 24, 26–33, 35–36,
    65, 93
Sovereignty, of Yahweh, 18–19, 22–23,
    27–30, 105
Spirit, of Yahweh, 88
Stager, Lawrence E., 96
Stairway, 59, 61, 63
Standing stone, Bethel, 64
Stargate, 3–4, 109
Strack, H. L., 122
Stuart, Douglas, 83, 88, 99
Stuhlmueller, Carroll, 22

T

Tabernacle, xi, 12–13, 24–25, 51–55,
    114–20, 128, 130–32, 134–35, 137
Tate, Marvin E., 103
Telegram, 8, 11, 39–55
Temple
    First Jerusalem, 24, 28–29, 106–8
    Second Jerusalem, 109, 111–12
    Shiloh, 76–77
Texting, 3
Theophany, 49, 74
To be cursed, meaning, 107–8
Togtman, Ray, 71
Tomlinson, Alan, 133
Tower of Babel, xvii, 7
Transcendence, of Yahweh, 21–22, 28–31

SCRIPTURE INDEX

169

2 Chronicles
3:6 *128*
5:2–6:11 *24*
6:6 *27*
6:18 *30*
7:14 *17*
7:16 *17*

Nehemiah
1:9 *17*

Job
4:16 *77*

Psalms
11:4 *118*
22:19 *131*
60:8 *44*
77:12 *48*
77:15 *48*
78 *104*
78:12 *48*
78:58–62 *103*
78:60 *104*
86:8 *30*
88:11 *48*
88:13 *48*
89:6 *48*
108:9 *44*
132:8 *104*
139:6 *48*

Isaiah
9:5 *48*
19:19–20 *62*
25:1 *48*
28:16 *133*
42:8 *17*
46:13 *131*
48:9 *17*

Jeremiah
7 *xi, 8, 13, 106–7*
7:10 *17*
7:12 *109*
7:12–15 *105*
7:14 *8, 109*

26 *106–7*
26:4–9 *106*
31:31–34 *124*
41:5 *104*
44:26 *17*
48:13 *102*

Ezekiel
8–11 *109*
9–10 *59*
20:9 *17*
20:14 *17*
20:22 *17*
20:44 *17*
36:23 *17*
40–48 *129*

Daniel
6:11 *35*
10 *61*

Hosea
4:13–14 *85*
4:15 *82*
8:1 *84*
8:5 *98*
9 *84*
9:9 *84*
9:15 *83, 85–86*
10 *98*
10:5 *98–99*
10:8 *99*
10:14 *100*
10:15 *100*
11:2 *85*
12:4–5 *100*
12:11 *85*
13:2 *85*

Joel
2 *127*
2:28 *127*

Amos
3:14 *101*
4:4 *87, 101*
5:4 *87*

5:5 *83, 87–88*
5:5–6 *101*
5:6 *87*
7:10–13 *101*
7:10–17 *82, 101*
8:14 *83, 87–89*

Haggai
2:8 *128*

Zechariah
1:9–17 *61*
7:2 *102*

Malachi
1:6 *17*
1:11 *17*
4:2 *17*

Matthew
9:20–22 *115*
27:46 *33*
27:51 *125*

Mark
15:34 *33*

John
1 *113, 120*
1:9–14 *113*
1:14 *114–15, 132*
1:43–51 *119*
1:50 *119*
1:51 *119*
2 *124*
2:13–17 *120*
2:18–22 *120*
2:19 *121, 132*
2:21 *120–21*
3:13 *120*
4 *124, 131*
4:19–26 *121*
14:8 *125*
14:15–26 *132*
14:18 *125*
14:26 *126*
20:12 *116*

20:15 *116*
20:19 *126*
20:22 *126*

Acts
2 *127*
2:3 *127*
23:6 *128*

1 Corinthians
3:9 *128*
3:9–17 *127*
3:10 *128*
3:12 *129*
3:16 *129*
3:16–17 *129*
6:9 *129*
8:7 *129*

2 Corinthians
13:5 *129*

Ephesians
2:11–19 *130*
2:11–22 *130*
2:17 *133*
2:18 *131*
2:19 *131–32*
2:20 *132*
2:20–22 *130–32*
3:9–10 *133*

Hebrews
9:1–5 *117*
9:6–10 *117*
9:11–25 *117*
9:23–25 *118*
12:12 *85*

1 Peter
2:6 *133*

Revelation
21:1–6 *131*
21:22 *134*
21:22–27 *131*